SCANDAL
ANNUAL
1993

By The Paragon Project

SCANDAL

ANNUAL

1993

Who Got Caught Doing
What in 1992

ST. MARTIN'S PRESS   NEW YORK

ISBN 0-312-929366

First Edition: December 1992

10 9 8 7 6 5 4 3 2 1

To our wonderful family—Bill, Val, Marty, Gloria, Jerry, Terri, Debbie, Betty, Norman, Kathy, David, Lucy, Jamie, Beth, Erin, Kate, Stephen, Don, and, of course, Ryan T.

CONTENTS

INTRODUCTION

"It showed that rumors about him are true—that he's an idiot."

> —Sixth-grader William Figueroa, who was at the blackboard when the Vice President of the United States tried to convince him that "potatoe" is the proper spelling for potato

Out of the mouths of babes comes the pure, unadulterated truth—and, as we at The Paragon Project have been pointing out for five long years, Dan Quayle should spend his days sitting in the corner of his White House office with a dunce cap on his head. But seeing the Vice President publicly boiled and mashed over this "potatoe" incident brings us decidedly mixed emotions—the sort of feelings you'd get watching your mother-in-law drive over the edge of a cliff in your brand-new Lexus.

On the one hand, we're thrilled that the entire country

finally realizes that Dan Quayle is the kind of man whose ineptitude has filled entire chapters in *Scandal Annual*. On the other hand, we're filled anew with the horror that this same man was just a heartbeat (a sometimes irregular heartbeat) away from the Presidency. What if he had gone to the United Nations, putter in hand, to talk about the Persian Golf Crisis? What if he'd asked Congress for a Declaration of Whore? In the end, however, we put aside these emotions and concentrated, as usual, in simply presenting the Vice President's gaffes for your entertainment.

And fortunately, for your added delight, we're also able to present the cornucopia of other political misdeeds and misstatements that always enliven an election year. From check kiting to backbiting, from Bill Clinton to H. Ross Perot, all the juicy quotes and stories are in *Scandal Annual 1993*.

As great as this material is, politics still had to share center scandal stage with the British royal family. The "warring Windsors" nabbed tabloid headlines around the world for weeks as the marriages of Prince Charles and Princess Di, Prince Andrew and the Duchess of York, and Princess Anne and Mark Phillips were either rocked or disintegrated, as purported by rumors of behavior that would have made Henry VIII blush. We think Queen Elizabeth could make a fortune syndicating a true-life soap opera called "All My Cheating Children."

But, as in any year, the most fascinating scandals come from the often bizarre behavior of ordinary people whose names aren't household ones. Looking for the latest in "drug highs"? Just go to the grocery store, head for the produce aisle, and score a few bunches of carrots. Yes, that's right, Bugs Bunny may have been a junkie. Researchers have uncovered a group of people so addicted to carrots that they nibble up to five bunches a day and horde skin shavings in fear of some future disease that could wipe out their supply. Fortunately, it doesn't take sophisticated detection to locate these addicts—their skin turns orange.

Then there is the would-be Jesse James who walked into a bank, stuck his finger under his sweater to look like a gun, and told the teller that he'd blow her away if she didn't give him the money. She offered a wad of bills—and our criminal of the year took his hand out from under his sweater to reach for it. She laughed, then about seven people jumped on the robber and held him for the police.

In conclusion, we guarantee you'll find every human weakness and foible of the famous and not-so-famous in this fun-packed seventh annual edition of *Scandal Annual.*

SCANDAL
ANNUAL
1993

1

SCANDALOUS QUOTES OF 1992

THEIR LAWN WAS A SHADE OF MURPHY BROWN . . .

I'll say one thing: Their lawn has never looked better. The Quayles never took care of it when they lived here.

> —*Newsweek* magazine quoting an unidentified neighbor of the Virginia home Dan Quayle rented to a single mother, her two kids, and her boyfriend

CASTING THE FIRST STONE

You can't compete with a pet rock.

> —Dee Dee Myers, Bill Clinton's press secretary, on the Ross Perot phenomenon

GOD COMMUNICATES THROUGH VANNA!

The weirdest thing was the television set was on, and that show with Vanna White was on, "Wheel of Fortune," and you know what the phrase was that she was turning the letters over for? "Miscarriage of Justice."

> —Defense attorney Kathleen A. Behan, describing her last meeting with Roger Keith Coleman, just before his execution in Virginia for a crime many people believed he didn't commit

DO WHAT I SAY, NOT WHAT I DO

These greenies have nice speeches, but in practice they're pigs.

> —A janitor at the Rio Earth Summit, while sweeping up streamers, wrappers, paper cups, and other debris after a meeting on waste management

THE *TITANIC* HAD A GREAT CRUISE, EXCEPT FOR THE ICEBERG

It's been a very good trip, with the exception of the tear gas.

> —White House press spokesperson Marlin Fitzwater, on the trip to Panama during which President Bush was forced to abandon a public appearance when an anti-American protest rally got out of hand

HOW ABOUT FORMING A JOINT COMMITTEE?

As one of the few politicians who admits to both having inhaled and having enjoyed it, of course I support it.

> —Congressman Joe Kennedy, on using
> marijuana for medicinal purposes

LUKE, THE GIRLY MAN?

I'm very in touch with my feminine side. Women don't always want to be manhandled. A lot of times they want to be made love to by a man who can do it softly, like a woman.

> —"Beverly Hills, 90210" star Luke Perry

WELL, IT WOULD FAZE US

I could stand nude in the middle of Madison Square Garden now and I don't think it would faze me.

> —Sharon Stone

YOU AND LUKE MIGHT BE A MATCH. . . .

Macho guys might feel threatened by me.

> —Michael Bolton

MADONNA IN THE RUDE

I met her. She's been to my house and she's rude. That's it. She's rude because she can be, because she can get away with it. She wasn't rude to me, but she was rude to everybody else. I thought, It's stupid but she's young. Being rude like that is just immature shortsightedness.

> —Cher

SIZING UP HER GRASS?

Her face. Then her backyard.
—Emilio Estevez, on what he notices
first about a woman

DEJA RUE

I'd lock myself in a cage, swallow the key, and hope for constipation.
—Traci Lords, an actress and ex-teen
porno movie star, on what she'd do if
she were 15 again

SPOKEN LIKE A TRUE MULTIMILLIONAIRE

Nonsense. Whose life would you rather have? What Bill Clinton goes through or what I go through?
—Arnold Schwarzenegger, putting the
kabash on reports he's thinking about
running for the U.S. Senate

THE ROLLING PARENT

Children have to go through a period of going crazy. I mean, of course, you don't want it to end in death. That's kind of the limit, death. You don't want it to go that far.
—Mick Jagger

THE NAKED TRUTH

I think I have my best moments when I'm nude, asleep in my bed. Now that I think about it, I have my most sensual thoughts in bed, my most creative thoughts in the bathroom, and when I'm in the shower, I come to conclusions about myself.

—Drew Barrymore

CLASH OF THE TITANS, VOLUME 1

I was a big fat pig. . . . I weighed 320 pounds. . . . I was uncomfortable and we were unable to have sex.

—Roseanne Arnold, on why she and her husband dieted

CLASH OF THE TITANS, VOLUME 2

We had sex, but it wasn't as good, you know, if you're that much further away, if you've got a big gut, you know, every inch counts.

—Tom Arnold

FAIR-WEATHER FRIEND

Things change.

—A White House official, on why President Bush snubbed Los Angeles police chief Daryl Gates, a former political ally, on his trip to L.A. after the riots

D-U-M-B-E

I wonder who wrote all those long words for him.
> —New York Governor Mario Cuomo,
> after Dan Quayle called him
> "liberalism's sensitive philosopher-
> king"

OKAY, MIKE, YOUR TURN TO BE THE WIFE

I'm in trouble because I'm normal and slightly arrogant. A lot of people don't like themselves and I happen to be totally in love with myself.
> —Mike Tyson, from the slammer

HEAR THAT, DOCTOR RUTH?

We've got to protect family life. We cannot protect family life if we have people going around proclaiming what they do in the bedroom, whether it's heterosexual or homosexual. It's just traveling a pathway to anarchy.
> —An Alexandria, Virginia, man on why
> he filed a complaint against a new gay
> bar in town

THE SORES OF TRIPOLI

I hope the sheets have been changed.
> —Israeli Prime Minister Yitzhak
> Shamir, after being told that the bed
> he had used in Bulgaria had been
> slept in by Libyan leader Muammar
> al-Qaddafi

A MAN WHO LOVES HIS WORK

What makes me feel psychologically good is when I am putting the rope around the convict's neck, I hear him muttering his last words, "Forgive me, God. Forgive me, God." These words indicate he is guilty.

—Egyptian state executioner
Helmi Sultan

YOU RANG?

Well, excuse me, George Herbert irregular-heart-beating, read-my-lying-lipping, sipping-in-the-pool, do-nothing, deficit-raising, make-less-money-than-Millie-the-White-House-dog-last-year, Quayle-loving, sushi-puking Walker Bush.

—Arsenio Hall, after White House press
spokesperson Marlin Fitzwater said
that President Bush would accept an
invitation to appear on any talk show
except his

THE MICKEY MOUSE THAT ROARED

When I look at a film of Kevin Costner's, I fall asleep out of boredom.

—Mickey Rourke

HAND JOBS FOR EVERYONE!

A little, but I talked to him and told him he could star in the next film, so he was okay.

—Magician Christopher Hart, on
whether his left hand was jealous of
his right hand's starring role as Thing
in *The Addams Family* movie

AS LONG AS THEY SPELL MY NAME RIGHT . . .

But it's not as good as Warren Beatty's baby! I wish I had thought of that.

> —Bette Midler, on the publicity she received from Geraldo Rivera's description of sex with her in his autobiography

DOESN'T SOUND BAD TO US

I am a rock cliché. I have fallen to every cliché a rock guy's supposed to do. I do have a Porsche. My girlfriend is a model. I couldn't admit this would ever happen to me, but guess what, it did.

> —John Mellencamp

YOU HAVEN'T SUNK *THAT* LOW

Hurt my image? What am I? A politician?

> —Keanu Reeves, on playing a male prostitute in *My Own Private Idaho*

NO HAUSFRAU

I don't know what I'm supposed to base myself on. When do I have to cut my hair and quit wearing jeans and my leather jacket and going on motorcycle rides? When do I have to start wearing a bun and stay home?

> —Cher

WAIT TILL YOU SEE HIS "HAMLET"!

Oh, Jesus, I didn't want to do *Home Alone*, but they kept offering me more money.

—Joe Pesci

PERFECT INEPTITUDE

The beautiful thing about this is everybody contributed.

—Manager of the Peninsula Pilots baseball team after the team's record twentieth straight loss

SIGN OF THE TIMES

We are sorry for any temporary inconvenience.

—Sign posted by Ukraine officials on a statue of Lenin that had not yet been demolished

THE COMPASSIONATE POLITICIAN OF THE YEAR AWARD

What a great savings!

—Former Chilean dictator Gen. Augusto Pinochet, when he learned that the people killed in his 1973 coup had been buried two to a coffin

KEEPING DAD ABREAST

I thought she was going to pursue a career in journalism.

—Talbot D'Alemberte, president of the American Bar Association, on learning that his daughter Gabrielle would pose topless in *Playboy*

COME AGAIN?

Will had to reluctantly admit that was true, which has certainly helped him with dates since then.

> —Roy Black, attorney for William
> Kennedy Smith, joking about his
> client's claim that he had sex twice in
> 30 minutes with Patricia Bowman

SENTIMENTAL SLAYER

You don't forget your first one.

> —Serial killer Jeffrey Dahmer, on why
> he would remember so many details
> about his first victim

THE ULTIMATE NIGHTMARE

What we would have is the combination of the compassion of the IRS and the efficiency of the post office.

> —Secretary of Health and Human
> Services Louis Sullivan, on what
> would happen if the health-care
> system was nationalized

DOES DANNY THINK HE'S JESUS?

We've long had hopes of converting Leonard Bernstein to the Republican Party. But it's about time to give up.

> —A spokesman for Dan Quayle, after
> learning the V.P. had recently sent a
> fund-raising letter to Bernstein, who
> had died more than a year previously

LA DUCE VITA

Until recently the word *fascist* was considered shameful. Fortunately, that period has passed. In fact, there is a reassessment of how much Grandpa Benito did for Italy.

> —Alessandra Mussolini, granddaughter of Benito Mussolini, at the start of her successful campaign for a seat in the Italian parliament

SCARFACE HEADS IBM?

Basically, it's the same exact talent. Sales is sales.

> —A former marijuana smuggler who now works for a company that produces ecologically sound products

MONKEY BUSINESS

The problem is that there aren't that many videos showing gorillas having sex. If there were a porn video of gorillas, we'd really like to get our hands on it.

> —A Japanese veterinarian, after local zookeepers showed a film of gorillas mating to a female gorilla who isn't aroused by her partner

MALE CHAUVINIST OF THE YEAR

I am delighted with some of the women that our Republican Senate candidates are taking on because they will be easier to beat.

> —George Bush

THE CEMENT BUSINESS WOULD BE BOOMING

I would like to say emphatically that I am innocent. I am guilty, though. I am guilty of being a good friend of John Gotti. And if there were more men like John Gotti on this earth, we would have a better country.

> —Convicted mobster Frank (Frankie Locs) Loscascio, after he and John Gotti were sentenced to life in prison for murder and racketeering

ROSS THE TOTAL LOSS?

He is too immature to be entrusted with the leadership responsibilities inherent in sea duty.

> —Quote from a 1955 assessment of Ross Perot while he was serving in the U.S. Navy

YOU SAID IT!

The life of human beings is very short. We are all going to die. Why should we cling so much to power?

> —Algerian President Muhammad Boudiaf, seconds before he was assassinated

JUMPY JUMPY?

Who wants to chew gum with the wrapper on?

> —Zozo, a jumpy jumpy, as promiscuous men are called in East Africa, on why he won't wear a condom

THE CLEAR THINKING THAT BROUGHT THIS COUNTRY TO THE POINT AT WHICH IT IS TODAY

I see no media mention of it, but we entered in—you asked what time it is and I'm telling you how to build a watch here—but we had Boris Yeltsin here the other day. And I think of my times campaigning in Iowa, years ago, and how there was a—Iowa has kind of, I single out Iowa, it's kind of an international state in a sense and has great interest in all these things—and we had Yeltsin standing here in the Rose Garden, and we entered into a deal to eliminate the biggest and most threatening ballistic missiles . . . and it was almost, "How-hum, what have you done for me recently?"

> —George Bush, defending himself

RAISING ARIZONA

We're going to wrestle to the ground this gigantic orgasm that is just out of control.

> —Sen. Dennis DeConcini of Arizona,
> who evidently intended to use the
> word *organism* when discussing the
> proposed balanced-budget
> amendment

OF COURSE, NOW THAT YOU PUT IT THAT WAY . . .

We don't necessarily discriminate. We simply exclude certain types of people.

> —An ROTC lieutenant colonel, on the
> military's ban on homosexuals

BIRD BRAINS

If you took the brains of the majority of the Supreme Court and put them into the head of a bird, the bird would fly backwards forever and ever and ever.

—Benjamin Hooks, NAACP chairman,
on the Supreme Court

SHUT UP, MARILYN

Marilyn, we had a hard enough time getting Bobby here tonight. If you're going to give him a hard time, do it in your own home, not mine.

—Barbara Bush, after the V.P.'s wife
teased Dorothy Bush LeBlond's future
husband, Bobby Koch, because he's a
Democrat

YEAH, IT'S A SHAME ABOUT ALL THAT MONEY

Pop rapes you, uses everything you have; then you're stuck in no-man's-land.

—Garth Brooks

MORE GREAT MOMENTS IN SELF-IMPORTANCE

I wanted to say, "Who wouldn't be nervous being next to a big, big star like you?"

—Dennis Miller, on Shannen Doherty's
asking if she made him nervous

YOUR WIFE'S UGLY, TOO . . .

I figure it's a pretty sad commentary when you've got to lose sixty pounds to play Babe Ruth.

—John Goodman

WELL . . .

I wasn't drilling for procreation.

—Jack Nicholson, on the unplanned children he fathered with Rebecca Broussard

I AM WOMAN

If you have a vagina and a point of view, that's a deadly combination.

—Sharon Stone

GREAT MOMENTS IN INFERIORITY

I used to feel not just unimportant but like a black hole, worse than invisible, with everyone avoiding me as if afraid they'd get sucked in.

—Mercedes Ruehl

IT GIVES US THE CREEPY CRAWLIES, TOO

And my eyes are open and I'm talking, and all these bugs drop on my face. They went in my ears and my eyes, and I— who pride myself on having worked with gorillas and everything and being a good trooper—I went nuts. You realize what it's like to be naked and blind and have bugs thrown in your face?

—Sigourney Weaver, on the first day of shooting *Aliens III*

STAY IN IRAQ WHERE YOU BELONG

We are here to say to the government, "You've got enough problems of your own. Stay out of my womb!"
—Jane Fonda, at a pro-choice rally

YEAH, BUT WHAT IF ONE GROWS UP TO BE A PHOTOGRAPHER?

He's a rarity as a father. He's so there. . . . It's all about purity, honesty, and that cliché unconditional love. I always knew he was that way, though. He was that way with his dogs.
—Robin Wright, on her boyfriend, Sean Penn

CAN ANYONE STAND PAT?

I admire Ted Kennedy. How many 59-year-olds do you know who still go to Florida for spring break?
—Pat Buchanan

IF IGNORANCE IS BLISS, SHE'S THE HAPPIEST WOMAN ON EARTH

I didn't ask him for a résumé when I fell in love with him.
—Victoria Gotti, wife of alleged Mafia godfather John Gotti, claiming she doesn't know how her husband earns a living

ARAB-ISRAELI RELATIONS SEMINAR, LESSON ONE

The Jews at work! Damn their fathers! Dogs! Filthy! Dirt!
—PLO leader Yasir Arafat, allegedly
quoted after Israel tried to block the
admission of a radical Palestinian
leader into France for medical
treatment

THAT'S SOUTHERN-FRIED ASS

I'd like to thank my family for loving me and taking care of
me. And the rest of the world can kiss my ass.
—The last words of Johnny Frank
Garrett, executed in Texas for
murdering a Catholic nun in 1981

CROSS HIM OFF THE LIST FOR THE LEAGUE OF WOMEN VOTERS CONVENTION

The weakest nations in the world are those that had a woman
as a leader. It doesn't mean that Islam is against women. On
the contrary. It respects them and says they are equal to men.
But history shows that weak nations are lead by women.
—Afghanistan's interim President
Sibjhatullah Mojadedi, on why he
thinks a woman shouldn't lead an
Islamic government

SQUASH THAT BUG

She is a water bug on the surface of life.
—Gloria Steinem, on writer Sally
Quinn, who wrote that feminism is
perceived as a fringe cause "with
overtones of lesbianism and man-
hating"

JUST DOIN' MY JOB, AND PROUD OF IT

Just lucky, I guess.

> —The owner of Milwaukee's United
> Military Supply PEX, on how it felt to
> have sold a mallet to serial killer
> Jeffrey Dahmer and a knife to a man
> who recently stabbed his wife to
> death

WHERE IS THE PRESIDENTIAL SENSE OF HUMOR?

I might start by recommending that you put "Doonesbury" in the obituary section; that might make a contribution.

> —George Bush, responding to a question
> at a newspaper publisher's meeting

HOW KATHY LEE GOT FRANK

I turn my back for two and a half hours on a Thursday afternoon. I look up. She has him out the checkout counter, out the door, bagged, and in her car. . . . I didn't even know what hit me.

> —Diane Sawyer, on Kathie Lee Gifford.
> Sawyer had been dating Frank Gifford
> when he met Kathie Lee.

SOMETHING WAS FISHY

I knew there was a big problem when we got reports of fish in basements.

> —The Chicago police superintendent, on
> the underground flood that caused
> hundreds of millions of dollars of
> damage in the downtown business
> district

NOT TO MENTION THE LESBIAN BIKER NUNS

You can no longer just put prostitutes on. It has to be prostitutes who are sex addicts.
> —A producer for "Donahue," on the
> competition in the daytime talk-show
> market

YOU OVER THERE. DROP 'EM!

Let's just say this is a unique case.
> —A Toledo, Ohio, detective, after
> $108,000 worth of glow-in-the-dark
> panties were stolen from a warehouse

OH, WELL, YEAH, EXCEPT FOR THAT

Restaurants are the place they can relax, where they can associate with each other. It's always been a safe haven—except, perhaps, when they get killed.
> —Gay Talese, on why mobsters like to
> hang out in restaurants

DOES THIS MAKE YOU FEEL OLD?

Who is she?
> —Casey Weldon, all-American
> quarterback for Florida State, when
> told he was going to meet Ringo Starr

STIFF UPPER LIP

It was so hard on the daffodils.
> —-Margaret Thatcher, after an angry
> woman whacked her on the head with
> a bunch of flowers

WARREN, SOFT AND GOOEY

Grumple Munchkee. It's been shortened to Munch and to Bubble-Gurble.
> —Warren Beatty, when asked if he and
> Annette Bening have a nickname for
> their infant daughter, Kathlyn

DID WARREN GET TRAPPED?

Actually, no.
> —Annette Bening, on whether she was
> surprised to discover she was
> pregnant

IMPRESSIVE SELF-KNOWLEDGE

I respect a woman too much to marry her.
> —Sylvester Stallone

MORE SELF-CRITICISM

I hear songs of mine on the radio and think, Oh, my God, I am really sorry that's a hit record because I sure don't want to listen to it.
> —John Mellencamp

MONKEY BUSINESS

You take a bunch of talented chimpanzees and give them a bucket of paint and they'll destroy a Rembrandt or van Gogh. The critics who are insensitive, rude people can kiss my ass.

—Michael Bolton, backstage at the Grammys, after being told that hisses and boos were sounded in the press room when his award was announced

NO EXCUSE

I did it as a favor to someone. Not many people liked it, so I guess it wasn't a good move. Please don't hate me.

—Model Naomi Campbell, on why she appeared in the Vanilla Ice film *Cool as Ice*, which got terrible reviews

DOES SHE ALSO SLEEP WITH AN APE?

We're so alike.

—Elizabeth Taylor, on why she has a close friendship with Michael Jackson

NOSE NEWS

I'm blessed, frankly, with bad sinuses. I put up with the snot, because I got a great voice in exchange.

—Michael Stipe

OBVIOUSLY, IT'S NOT REAL LIFE

Unlike the show, the majority of cars are not Porsches and Corvettes. There are lots of BMWs and Jeeps.

> —A Beverly Hills High School student, on the difference between her school and the one portrayed in "Beverly Hills, 90210"

THE SENATOR RADIATES COMPASSION

You should draw a mushroom cloud and put underneath it, "Made in America by lazy and illiterate Americans and tested in Japan."

> —South Carolina Sen. Ernest Hollings, suggesting in a speech how atom bombs should be labeled

ON REPUBLICAN MEN

If George Bush reminds many women of their first husbands, Pat Buchanan reminds women why an increasing number of them are staying single.

> —Ohio University communications professor Judy Pearson

SO GIVE THEM A SPEEDING TICKET

Where's the fire?

> —A Libyan fire fighter, who showed up at the Venezuelan Embassy in Tripoli before a supposedly spontaneous mob arrived to set it on fire

THE KING EATS FEWER DORITOS

We've been trying to get Elvis. He's been dead long enough.
>—Ray Foreman, brother of the geriatric
>wonder boxer George, on his sibling's
>next opponent

SO DIANA DARLINK, VAT DO YOU THINK OF HIS PENIS?

If they would come to my office, I really do believe I could help them.
>—Dr. Ruth Westheimer, on the marital
>troubles of Charles and Diana

A RARE HONEST POLITICIAN

That's a good question. Let me try to evade you.
>—Paul Tsongas, when asked if he's more
>interested in promoting his own views
>than in helping Bill Clinton win the
>Presidency

JUST WHAT WE NEED, A 14-YEAR-OLD VICE PRESIDENT

He seems like an average type of man. He's not, like, smart. I'm not trying to rag on him or anything. But he has the same mentality I have—and I'm in the eighth grade.
>—A 14-year-old girl, after Dan Quayle
>visited her South-central Los Angeles
>school

IT'S ALWAYS THE ONE THAT GOT AWAY

Some older men may say their erections aren't as big as they recall them once being. But then their partner says, "Well, dear, you overestimated them back then, too."

> —A psychologist at the National
> Institute on Aging, speaking about the
> concept of male menopause

WE UNDERSTAND

That's M-A-D-E, not M-A-I-D.

> —Whoopi Goldberg, making sure the
> title of her upcoming movie wasn't
> misinterpreted during a discussion of
> racism

TAKE THOSE VALUES, DANNY

If the Vice President thinks it's disgraceful for an unmarried woman to bear a child, and if he believes that a woman cannot adequately raise a child without a father, then he had better make sure abortion remains safe and legal.

> —Diane English, producer of "Murphy
> Brown," after Quayle criticized the
> show for glorifying unwed
> motherhood

KOON HAS MANDINGO COMPLEX

He grabbed his butt with both hands and began to shake and gyrate his fanny in a sexually suggestive fashion. As King sexually gyrated, a mixture of fear and offense overcame Melanie. The fear was of a Mandingo sexual encounter.

> —L.A. Police Sgt. Stacey Koon,
> acquitted in the Rodney King case,
> describing how he and Officer Melanie
> Singer viewed the incident

DUCK, AL!

I think I'm going to throw. I think I'm going to hurl chunks.
> —Madonna, after Tipper Gore came over to introduce herself at a film premiere

DANNY—PRO AND CON

I think Dan Quayle—I don't expect any of you to agree with this—I think he's got the best political mind in the White House.
> —Massachusetts Republican Gov. William Weld

Are you kidding me?
> —White House Political Director Ronald Kaufman, responding to Weld's remark

I'LL HAVE A TRIPLE EAGLEBURGER WITH CHEESE

First of all, it was ego. And secondly, I wanted to screw up the Social Security system.
> —Deputy Secretary of State Lawrence Eagleburger, on why he named each of his three sons Lawrence

DEADLY "TO DO" LIST

2:30 open window, 3:15 dispose of body, 3:45 be home making out.
> —From instructions allegedly written by a 16-year-old boy charged in the brutal murder of his girlfriend's mother

PSST, DAN, YOU AND GEORGE ARE THE INCUMBENTS THIS TIME

We will be asking them to join with us. I'm going to ask them to help us to change the Congress. It's not just enough to change the President if you want to change America.

> —Dan Quayle, on courting Ross Perot supporters

POLITICAL GAS AND ELECTRIC

Stop the power of the few.

> —Jerry Brown, demanding an end to the influence of special-interest groups while being honored at a champagne breakfast paid for by Arco and Southern California Edison

WE SYMPATHIZE

The worst thing is that I had to read *On Wings of Eagles* for nothing.

> —*Washington Post* reporter David von Deehle, after Ross Perot dropped out of the Presidential campaign

SAY "AH"

It's not good for business if you care for a second whether blood is bubbling from a guy's mouth.

> —Minnesota Vikings star Joey Browne, on playing defense in the NFL

SOUNDS LIKE POLITICS

Things were run on a need-to-know principle: If you needed to know, you weren't told.

> —Peter Jay, a former top executive in the business empire of the late Robert Maxwell, which was plunged into scandal after Maxwell's mysterious death

WIPE THAT SMILE OFF YOUR FACE

He saw Oswald come out with a smirk on his face and that ticked him off.

> —Earl Ruby, on why his brother Jack Ruby shot and killed Lee Harvey Oswald

TED TURNER, TSAR

Your empire is doing well now? It's not being dismantled?

> —Mikhail Gorbachev, to CNN president Tim Johnson

TIRED OF CHINESE FOOD?

I guess for a high-fashion restaurant like this, the prices are okay.

> —A Chinese college student, at the opening of the new Bejing McDonald's

AND THAT'S MUCH TOO SOON

I'll see you in a million years.

> —An Eatonton, North Carolina, child to convicted child molester Robert F. Kelley, Jr., who was sentenced to 12 consecutive life terms

YEAH, BUT SHE HAD A BETTER YEAR

Study hard and you might grow up to be President. But let's face it, even then you'll never make as much money as your dog.

> —George Bush, talking to high school students after learning his dog Millie earned $889,176 in book royalties

IS DAN QUAYLE DISEASE CATCHING?

My position has not changed. I am, uh, pro-, pro-, uh, pro-life.

> —George Bush, on abortion

LET US PREY

I'm trying to let this thing die.

> —A West Richland, Washington, Baptist pastor on why he doesn't discuss the fact that he once served time for strangling his wife and choking his female companion, whom he left for dead

SURE, PEEWEE

They actually had to reinforce the underwear several times so there wouldn't be any unsightly bulges.

> —Model Darren MacBee, after posing as
> Samson for an underwear commercial

I RUV WHAT 'CHEW DO FOR ME

I just wanted to get a little attention.

> —George Bush, after vomiting on
> Japanese Prime Minister Kiichi
> Miyazawa

BROTHERLY LOVE

There's nothing much more important this year than the reelection of our great United States Senator Alfonse D'Amato.

> —Jonathan Bush, whose brother George
> is also running for reelection

SOMEHOW, THIS SEEMS ILLOGICAL

Doctor Kevorkian doesn't support the death penalty.

> —Attorney for the physician called Dr.
> Death, on why his client wouldn't
> allow his suicide machine to be used
> by a convicted felon serving a life
> sentence

LOW BLOW

Because I don't have a friend who's willing to pose nude for a girlie magazine.

> —Oliver North, on why he couldn't compete for the seat of Virginia Sen. Chuck Robb, who allegedly had a dalliance with a *Playboy* model

FIRM NIPPLES AT *THE NEW YORKER*

If it makes Tina's nipples firm, she goes with it.

> —A *Vanity Fair* writer, on then-editor Tina Brown, who has since taken over as editor-in-chief of the much more staid *New Yorker* magazine

THE DAZE OF WHINE AND ROSES

Either you're in the "in" club or the "out" club. I was always out. It hasn't changed over forty years.

> —Dustin Hoffman, on being a high school outcast

MORK FROM DORK

I couldn't imagine living the way I used to live. Now people come up to me from the drug days and go, "Hi, remember me?" And I'm going, "No, did I have sex with you? Did I take a dump in your toolbox?"

> —Robin Williams

FAMILIAR TARGET

This means I have to insult someone, doesn't it? Well then, Barry Manilow.

> —Lisa Stansfield, on what would be her "duet from hell"

VIEW FROM THE FRONT

It would be my guess that Madonna is not a very happy woman. From my own experience, having gone through persona changes like that, that kind of clawing around to be the center of attention is not a pleasant place to be.

> —David Bowie

OKAY, YOU CAN PUT AWAY THE LYSOL

As far as I'm concerned, sex ruins almost everything. Madonna feels this even more strongly than I do. We have spoken about it a lot and she is very down on sex at the moment.

> —Sandra Bernhard

NOT MADE IN HEAVEN

Because we're fucking stupid. It's like an occupational hazard.

> —Gary Oldman, on why actors marry actresses

LIKE, WOW . . .

You have to sign all kinds of releases when you get to the gate that you won't tell anybody what happened. I mean, this is a big happening.

—Bo Derek, on being invited to Michael Jackson's ranch

STING WANTS TO BE BAD

You do get sick of being characterized as a do-gooder—maybe I'll start a campaign to destroy the rain forest.
—Sting

EVEN PARANOIDS HAVE ENEMIES

There's 1,001 vultures out there, crouched on their rocks, saying, "Ah, here comes Stone."
—Oliver Stone, on his critics

WILL WARREN AND ANNETTE BE FOREVER?

I have a feeling Warren Beatty is having a baby so he can meet babysitters.
—David Letterman

OLIVIER FELT THE SAME WAY

I'd rather dig a hole through the center of the earth with my tongue.

—Johnny Depp, on returning to television

I AM WHAT I AM

I'm a meathead. I can't help it, man. You've got smart people and you've got dumb people.
—Keanu Reeves

WE KNOW WHAT YOU MEAN

In my young days, I used to pick up sluts, and I don't mean that nastily. It's more a term of endearment, really, for girls who know how to speak their minds.
—Kevin Costner

ROSE BOWLING

If I was as ugly as Axl Rose, I'd be pissed off about cameras going off in my face, too.
—Ted Nugent, Damn Yankees guitarist, on a riot in St. Louis that started when Rose leaped off the stage to grab a fan's camera

BROKEN AXL

I know people are confused by a lot of what I do, but I am, too, sometimes.
—Axl Rose

LOVE ON CAMERA

They spend so much time beforehand doing things like covering the zits on your ass, that during the actual scene, you're numb. It's over before you know it. All I remember is feeling very good driving home that night.
—Brad Pitt, on his love scene with Geena Davis in *Thelma and Louise*

JACK, JR., ON BEING ACCUSED OF BEING JACK, JR.

If I make a move, like raise my eyebrows, some critic says I'm doing Jack Nicholson. What am I supposed to do, cut off my eyebrows?
> —Christian Slater

AND WHERE WOULD BEING AN *A* STUDENT HAVE GOTTEN HIM?

If James used the effort toward his studies that he uses to be humorous, he'd be an *A* student.
> —Jay Leno's fifth-grade report card

HEEL, GEORGE-SAN

This must be Bush's dog.
> —Sen. Bob Kerry, after a dog threw up at his feet

VICTORY IN THE WAR ON DRUGS

They've got the President to stop taking Halcion. That was this year's bright spot for the war on drugs.
> —A U.S. drug-enforcement official, joking about George Bush's use of sleeping pills

OH, SHUT UP, YOU OLD BORE!

I have never seen a professional baseball game, an episode of "Dallas," or of Roseanne Barr or of Geraldo Rivera or of the black lady who is alternately fat and thin. I forget her name.
> —William Buckley, countering charges that George Bush lacks the common touch

REALLY, WE'RE JUST LIKE THE AVERAGE GUY

I just can't wait until this campaign is over so I can say, "Bob, open the garage door and get out the Maserati! Open the safe and get out the jewels."

> —Georgette Mosbacher, wife of Robert Mosbacher, chairman of the Bush campaign, on the frugal lifestyle in election years

MEN ALWAYS BLAME THE WOMAN

The love scenes would just get hot, just get really hot, just start to really work—and she'd cut. And I would say, "Barbra! Why are you cutting this? This is just getting good."

> —Nick Nolte, on Barbra Streisand's direction in *The Prince of Tides*

GREAT MOMENTS IN RACIAL TOLERANCE

I forgot no one was working. Everyone had Buckwheat's birthday off.

> —A Mardela Springs, Maryland, town commissioner, on why he had trouble contacting county employees on Martin Luther King Day

CAPITAL SWINE

The really scary thing is that some of these people work for the government.

> —Washington Redskins lineman Joe Jacoby, on fans who attend the games wearing pig snouts

GENTLEMAN OF THE YEAR

Kim Basinger is the most self-indulgent, dumb, most irritating person I've ever met. She's as dumb as a shoe.

—Jonathan Van Meter, a *Vogue* writer

LICKING HIS WOUNDS

Graffiti Bridge was not a failure. Maybe it will take people thirty years to get it. They trashed the *Wizard of Oz* at first, too.

—Prince, on his movie that bombed at the box office

WE COULDN'T HAVE SAID IT BETTER

A grunting, voracious pig in heat.

—Geraldo Rivera, describing his younger self in his autobiography

IT WAS VATS OF VASELINE

I was never into notches on the belt, but going out for the evening was pretty easy. Still, there were never fourteen girls swinging from chandeliers into vats of Crisco.

—Michael J. Fox, on his bachelor days

GEE, WE'D NEVER KNOW BY LOOKING AT YOU

I'm a little insane. I hated my parents. And I'm just a hair away from being a serial killer.

—Dennis Hopper, on his many bizarre roles

I ENJOY BEING A GIRL

I've been with great men, real interesting men. . . . Men were always interested in me. There were certainly a lot of girls prettier or more available or friendlier, but I just love men. And they like to have me around.

—Jessica Lange

YOU MEAN YOU CAN'T BELIEVE WHAT YOU READ?

Sometimes they take one line out of context. Like if I said, "I beat my dad in golf," they take out "in golf" and say, "I beat my dad." I mean, I've been "pregnant" so many times! I ate too much, so excuse me.

—Princess Stephanie, on tabloid journalism

A LITTLE RESENTFUL, DAVE?

I hate waiting in lines, but I'd do it.

—David Letterman, passed over for the "Tonight" show job, on whether he'd like to firebomb NBC

SURE CURE FOR YOUR NOSTALGIA ABOUT THE REAGAN DAYS

What's Nintendo?

—Former President Ronald Reagan, to a teenage hospital patient who asked him if he ever played the game

SHUT UP AND *DRINK,* YOU LITTLE TWERP!

I'm not crazy about the stuff. But money is money.
>—Macaulay Culkin, on signing a
>lucrative deal to endorse Sprite

SOMEHOW, WE GUESSED IT

I'm so excited to meet you. I've always modeled myself after Ginger.
>—Marla Maples, upon meeting actress
>Tina Louise, who played Ginger on
>"Gilligan's Island"

SURE, BUT HOW DO YOU THINK FERDINAND FEELS?

My dreams have become puny with the reality my life has become.
>—Imelda Marcos

ONLY IF THERE'S JUSTICE IN THE UNIVERSE

I figure in his next life he'll come back as a slug and someone will put salt on him and that will be the end of him.
>—A Virginia woman on Donald Trump,
>while attending a book signing by
>Ivana Trump

BAWDY BRADY

Almost from day one, my feelings toward Florence were more carnal than maternal.
>—Barry Williams, who played Greg
>Brady, on Florence Henderson, who
>played his mother on "The Brady
>Bunch"

WHAT ABOUT PEOPLE WHO INVADE OTHER COUNTRIES?

Those who dare to bomb an organization or plant a car bomb or break into a house to steal, killing the owner . . . should be beheaded or hanged as a warning.

> —Uday Saddam Hussein, eldest son of Iraqi President Saddam Hussein, calling for a return to public executions

LIEN ON YOUR COFFIN

Please provide your date of death.

> —A letter from the IRS addressed to a dead man whose widow filed a return for him

NO BELGIAN WAFFLE

In Europe, extramarital affairs are considered a sign of good health, a feat.

> —A Belgian legislator, commenting on the rumors swirling around Bill Clinton

THE JAPANESE PRIME MINISTER ASKED THE SAME QUESTION

Where were you when I needed you?

> —A message signed by President Bush, to SmithKline Beecham, the drug firm that makes the antinausea drug he took after vomiting on the Japanese Prime Minister

FLOWERS IN THE ATTIC

We're both victims of the prom-queen syndrome. I got over it with the first wrinkle, but Gennifer is still reaching for that tiara.

> —Joy Howland, a former friend of
> Gennifer Flowers, on their partying
> days in the 1980s when they were
> called the Gruesome Twosome

SOUNDS LIKE YOU WERE ROBIN WILLIAMS'S TWIN

I was cocaine addicted. I was an alcoholic. I had a sexual addiction. I was bulimic for six years. . . . I could be unbelievably horrible and stupid. . . . I'd walk out of a hotel suite because I didn't like the color of the bedspread. I remember looking out of my room at the Inn on the Park in London one day and saying, "It's too windy. Can someone do something about that?"

> —Elton John, on his life before recovery

BEAUTIFUL VIEW, BUTT . . .

One beautiful moment was skiing the Matterhorn, which I did for the first time a few months ago. I found it highly spiritual, although my butt hurt like hell after I was through.

> —Singer Chaka Khan, asked about her
> favorite things

HAVE YOU SEEN THIS ONE?

I'm a man that knows every hand gesture you've ever seen, and I haven't learned a new one since I've been here.

> —President Bush, on protesting
> Australian farmers who dogged him
> during his trip Down Under

MOST GUYS WOULD WILT

Look at Wilt Chamberlain. He says he slept with 20,000 women, and everyone thinks that's funny. If a woman had done that, I mean, why didn't someone just say to him, "You're a disgusting pig"? And these men who say they were only giving women what they wanted, that women are conspirators hanging around hotel lobbies waiting to trap men— excuse me, 6-foot, 9-inch, 280-pound man, maybe you have some responsibility in this.

> —Robin Givens

HUDSON SCHMUCK

I see her naked every day.

> —Bruce Willis, on his reaction to his wife Demi Moore's appearing nude on the cover of *Vanity Fair*

2

NOW, THAT'S
A CRIME

BITE COURT

Usually, the criminal justice system puts the bite on crimi-
nals, but a 44-year-old Pittsburgh man turned the tables
during his trial. After pleading guilty to assault, the man was
awaiting sentencing in an Allegheny County court when he
suddenly stood up, ran to the bench, and bit the judge on the
right temple. So he could go to the hospital for 14 stitches,
the judge deferred sentencing his attacker.

HE'S SUPPOSED TO HAVE AN APPLE
ON HIS HEAD, STUPID

A 25-year-old man, angry after an argument with his 28-year-
old male roommate and lover, waited until he fell asleep,
took out a hunting bow, and fired into the sleeper's skull. The
arrow entered the back of the head and penetrated so deeply

that the arrowhead popped out of the forehead. He was stringing another arrow for a second shot when the victim miraculously awoke and called the police. After a two-hour operation to remove the arrow, the survivor commented, "This is so bizarre."

FAIR'S FAIR

A pair of would-be thieves smashed a Burdines department store window in Miami Beach, Florida, grabbed all the clothing on display, tossed it into the backseat of their car, then sped away. In his haste, though, the driver lost control and crashed the car. A few minutes later, the bandits watched helplessly as a crowd of 75 people looted the stolen clothes from their car.

RULE 1: ALWAYS HIDE THE BODY

A 23-year-old Nashua, New Hampshire, man discovered that not paying for automobile body work can be more expensive than putting it off. The lesson came after a woman walking through an amusement-park parking lot noticed a black Jeep that had the exact same dents as a red Jeep stolen from her three weeks before. She walked over and tried her keys—to discover that they fit. She called the cops, who arrested the driver for possession of stolen property.

ANIMAL LOVER

A 35-year-old Pompano Beach, Florida, man was given the heave-ho by his girlfriend. Evidently, that made him more than a little mad, for he allegedly broke into her house, killed her pet birds, stole her cat, and stomped her daughter's bunny to death. The cops charged him with theft and cruelty to animals. We haven't been able to confirm reports that Saddam Hussein wants to name this guy Minister of Defense.

A SHARP REQUEST

Most of us have used creative tactics to weasle money out of Mom or Dad. But a 22-year-old Raleigh, North Carolina, man decided on the direct approach. He grabbed a knife from the kitchen, held it to his mother's throat, took her to an automatic-teller machine, and forced her to withdraw $20. Then he brought her back home, figuring she'd forget the whole thing. Not! She called the police.

NO WYATT EARP, BUT A HELL OF A CONSIDERATE GUY

Dodge City, Kansas, has a long and storied history of famous law enforcers, but one of them will not be a 19-year-old jail guard who was arrested for letting out an inmate, then driving him to a sexual rendezvous with his 15-year-old girlfriend.

WHAT IF HE BREAKS OUT?

A 24-year-old man, convicted of robbing a San Diego–area bank, has demanded that the FBI clear his reputation. The reason: The FBI said the man resembles the Clearasil Bandit, an acne-scarred felon wanted in eight other bank jobs. The convicted robber not only denies robbing those other financial institutions, but he also maintains that the nickname "caused me mental duress and mockery from jail officers and other inmates." Until the blemish is erased from his record, the man is allegedly biding his time playing goalie on the prison dart-board team.

HOLIDAY ON ICE

We've heard of designated drivers and designated hitters, but only in Morehead, Kentucky, have we encountered a designated inmate. County prison officials were embarrassed when a tipster told them that a local man had been serving 16 days of a 30-day sentence imposed on his brother-in-law. Turns out the prison doesn't require a picture I.D. when somebody surrenders, so the brother-in-law had almost gotten away with paying the inmate to serve his time. But once caught, he had to serve the sentence from the beginning and the designated con was given a bill for $320 for his brother-in-law's 16 days of lodging.

SOMETHING OLD, NEW, STOLEN, AND BLUE

An 18-year-old Prestonburg, Kentucky, bride and her sister went on a shopping spree a few hours before her wedding, accumulating a wedding gown, a veil, white shoes, suits, shirts, ties, a dress for a flower girl, two cushions for ring bearers, a camera, and 10 rolls of film. The only slight problem was that they had allegedly stolen all the stuff from seven stores. The pair was finally nabbed when a supermarket manager caught them lifting food for the reception. P.S. The wedding went on anyway, presumably in less fancy clothes.

THEY SHOULD HAVE RENTED *SOUND OF MUSIC*

A 35-year-old Milwaukee, Wisconsin, man allegedly flew into a rage after he and his girlfriend spent New Year's Eve watching the vampire movie *Son of Darkness: To Die For II*. Police said the would-be Dracula threw knives around the apartment, cut his girlfriend's chest and ear with a broken beer bottle, then tried to drink blood from her wounds.

GREAT MOMENTS IN BURGLARY, VOLUME I

The idea, you see, is to break in, take the merchandise, then steal away quietly and unobtrusively. Evidently, a 40-year-old Huntington, Indiana, man hasn't got the hang of planning a quiet getaway. After allegedly entering a local beer distributor's warehouse, the man imbibed a few bottles, loaded up a forklift with more than 30 cases, climbed into the driver's seat, and headed for home. Evidently, he hadn't mastered the art of handling the vehicle, because his route was strewn with dumped and broken cases. Of course, people who spotted this master criminal called the cops, who hauled him in. By the way, Huntington is the hometown of another more famous genius—Dan Quayle.

HOLD THE PICKLE, THE MAYO, AND THE DRIVER

A 38-year-old St. Louis man was hungry after a long night of imbibing at his local tavern. He got into his car, drove until he spotted a drive-through window that looked like a Burger King, and barked his order for a burger and fries into the intercom. To his surprise, the guy at the other end of the intercom was the moonlighting booking clerk of the local police station. The cops soon had it their way, tossing the guy into the slammer for drunken driving.

GREAT MOMENTS IN LAW ENFORCEMENT

An Anchorage, Alaska, man was aquitted on charges of illegal salmon fishing after chagrined prosecuters admitted in court that someone had eaten all the evidence.

PARTY ANIMAL

A 43-year-old Suffolk County, New York, man was released from jail a few hours after being arrested for drunken driving. Not learning his lesson, he allegedly went straight to a gin mill, got loaded again, climbed back into his car, then weaved into the opposite lane to smash into another car head on. The other driver was killed, while the two-time drunk, who was not seriously injured, was arrested for homicide.

DRUNKEN WHEELING

A Bowling Green, Kentucky, man who was missing both legs was convicted of drunken driving for operating his motorized wheelchair on a public road.

NEXT TIME, HOW 'BOUT A HONDA?

An 81-year-old Winter Haven, Florida, man was arrested for allegedly murdering his 81-year-old wife with a hatchet, a rope, and a butcher knife because she refused to let him buy a Cadillac. The senior slayer told authorities he killed his wife on Monday but didn't call police until Tuesday because he wanted to make sure she was really dead.

FATHER'S DAY

A 14-year-old Los Angeles girl allegedly resented her father's interference in her romance with a 17-year-old boyfriend. She wrote in her diary that she had a plan to shoot, burn, and bury her father. Six days later, she carried out the plan. The father was drugged with sleeping pills, shot once in the head, and then burned. The 14-year-old girl was arrested. Her boyfriend and a 16-year-old girlfriend admitted to participating in the killing, according to an affadavit released by police.

THEY COULDN'T FIND A PLAYBOY BUNNY

Police in Boynton Beach, Florida, came under fire after the surfacing of a video of a camping trip that showed police officers drunk, naked, and pretending to have sex with a man in a rabbit costume. The tape also showed six officers beating and shooting a black mannequin with "nigger" written on it. The police union said there was nothing racist on the tape.

LET HER FINGERS DO THE WALKING

A 47-year-old Phoenix, Arizona, woman was sentenced to four and a half years in jail for plotting to kill her husband. Her problem was she evidently believed the ads that promised you could find everything in the Yellow Pages. She looked up the number of an outfit called Guns for Hire, dialed, and ordered a hit man to bump off her hubby. Problem was, Guns for Hire stages western shows for carnivals, etc.

ARMED ROBBER OF THE YEAR AWARD

This prestigious honor goes to a 17-year-old Crescent, Iowa, man who used a gun to hold up a convenience store, then shot himself in the thigh as he walked out with the loot.

PSST, WANNA SEE A GALL BLADDER?

Some people just can't resist showing off their collections. However, that can be a problem if your collection is a garbage bag full of human organs. A 23-year-old Costa Mesa, California, woman was arrested for murder after she showed such a bag to a male friend, who tipped police. Parts of an entire dismembered male body were found in the woman's apartment.

TOP COPS

A Riverside, California, woman was raped and beaten by an intruder when police refused to respond to her home alarm. The reason: The woman still owed the $25 alarm permit fee required by police.

LET'S ORDER OUT

A lot of professional food critics can be difficult to please, but none are quite as demanding as a 62-year-old Wichita, Kansas, man. One Saturday night, he told his 61-year-old girlfriend that he'd shoot her if dinner wasn't good. Evidently, the fried chicken and rice wasn't up to muster; he allegedly got up from the dinner table, got his gun, and made good on his threat.

RUDE AWAKENING

A Burbank, California, woman woke up one morning to the familiar presence of a man sleeping next to her. Then she realized that her husband was out of town on business. She crept out of bed, grabbed her infant daughter, and called the cops. Turned out the man was a local drunk who had wandered into the house, stripped off his clothes, and climbed into the king-size bed to sleep it off.

SOUNDS LIKE A JURY OF CONGRESSMEN

A 47-year-old man charged with sending threatening and obscene letters to German Olympic skating champion Katarina Witt petitioned the judge for a jury made up only of nymphomaniacs and atheists. He said only such a jury would be free of prejudice and hatred against him. The judge said no.

THAT OLD BLACK MAGIC

Fortunately for 46-year-old Richard Leno of Salem, Massachusetts, it was 1992, not 1692. Otherwise, he would have been burned at the stake after he was convicted of larceny and perjury for using witchcraft to bilk an heiress out of $500,000. Among Leno's bizarre deeds was branding the heiress's breast to show his dominance over her.

HISTORY COMES BACK TO HAUNT SCHOOL

Most of us who failed a high school course didn't like the experience, but not many of us hold the kind of grudge displayed by a 20-year-old dropout from Lindhurst High in Oliverhurst, California. Having failed a history class allegedly became an obsession of the man's for more than three years. Finally, he exploded, charging into the school carrying weapons and wearing camouflage gear and an ammo belt. He fired into three classrooms, killing three students and the teacher who had failed him. He held about 80 students hostage for eight and a half hours before surrendering.

OUR DUTIFUL DAUGHTER OF THE YEAR AWARD

The unanimous winner is a 40-year-old Portland, Oregon, woman who kidnapped her 82-year-old wheelchair-bound father, an Alzheimer's sufferer, from a nursing home, cut the labels from his clothing, stuck a note on the wheelchair giving a phony name, and abandoned him at a dog track in Coeur d'Alene, Idaho.

CHIP OFF THE OLD BLOCKHEADS

A Leavenworth, Kansas, couple was arrested on charges of felony murder and child abuse after the body of their 4-year-old retarded son was found encased in cement in a box on the back porch of the family home.

STOP PAMPERING CRIMINALS!

Despite strong protests, Arizona prison officials refuse to change their policy of bringing inmates to their execution wearing nothing but an adult diaper. Prison officials argue that cyanide gas used in the gas chamber could cling to the clothing of the deceased, endangering those removing the body. Opponents argue that California and Mississippi gas without incident condemned men who are fully dressed.

FATHER OF THE YEAR CANDIDATE

A Brooklyn, New York, father was babysitting his 22-month-old son when he allegedly grew enraged by the toddler's behavior. According to police, he took the boy to a local park, hurled him into the bushes, and left him. The boy survived a presumably terrifying night before searchers found him the next morning.

DOUBLE JEOPARDY

Sofyan Ali Saleh, a native of Yemen who became a permanent resident of the U.S. in 1982, was convicted of manslaughter in 1983 for killing another Yemeni man. He served eight years, then was released—only to face the death penalty for the same crime.

The reason is that Sofyan Ali Saleh was tried in abstentia in Yemen and convicted of murder, a crime for which Islamic law requires the death penalty. The U.S. Immigration and Naturalization Service is attempting to deport him to his native country as an undesirable alien, so Ali Saleh went to court to protest that his deportation would constitute double jeopardy. However, the court refused to intervene.

BLASTING THE BLASTERS

According to residents of a Phoenix, Arizona, trailer park, a 49-year-old man and his 39-year-old girlfriend tormented them by blasting the stereo at all hours. So the 94-year-old man who lived in the next trailer decided to do something about it. He rolled his wheelchair next door and blasted the couple with a shotgun. Authorities plea-bargained the first-degree murder charges so the geriatric slayer wouldn't face the death penalty. But his five-year prison sentence may turn out to be the same thing.

TEEN HIT PARADE

According to police, the four teenage grandchildren of a 63-year-old Houston, Texas, woman decided that Grandma had to go. So the 13-year-old grandson went out and recruited a 15-year-old girl who agreed to kill Grandma. The hit girl donned an all-black outfit, snuck into the woman's home one evening, and blew her away as she watched TV. The girl was sentenced to 22 years in jail, while the grandchildren received 15-year terms.

HIGHWAY TO HEAVEN

A Washington, D.C., man was a passenger in a car riding down Interstate 295 one night when he announced he "felt like killing someone." He rolled down the window, pointed his gun, and shot to death a 36-year-old woman riding with her husband in a passing car.

IT BEATS CHASING THAT GUY DOWN ON RTE. 295

A 36-year-old female bus driver was at the wheel of a vehicle holding 40 suburban Baltimore sixth-graders in the loading zone of the Maryland Science Center when a policewoman ordered her to move. She refused. The policewoman yanked this obviously hardened criminal out of the van, arrested her, strip-searched her, and tossed her in jail. The mayor of Baltimore later apologized.

FOR THIS IS MY BODY . . .

Police burst into the Plymouth, Indiana, home of a Roman Catholic priest as he was cutting up and burning pictures of nude young males. The officers arrested him on charges of child molesting after they came into the possession of a videotape of him having sex with a child. Police seized more videotapes and photographs of the priest. The Catholic Church has come under national criticism for concealing instances of priests sexually abusing children.

HE SHOULD HAVE READ HIS OWN BOOK

A white supremacist who wrote about how to kill blacks and cover it up was convicted of first-degree murder for gunning down a black Persian Gulf war veteran in a Jacksonville, Florida, parking lot.

GEORGE WASHINGTON'S WALLET STOLEN

That's right, someone picked the Father of our Country's wallet from a display case at the Old Barracks Museum in Trenton, New Jersey. Fortunately, the wallet was anonymously returned three weeks later. The thief may have discovered that the $1.66 in Colonial money inside couldn't buy crack.

SOUTH CAROLINA JUSTICE

A 32-year-old South Carolina woman charged her husband with marital rape. The evidence: a videotape that showed her hands and feet tied with rope and her eyes and mouth sealed with duct tape as her husband had sex with her. The woman is heard on the tape begging her husband not to tie her up. The tape also contains the sounds of slaps and muffled screams.

The husband's defense was that the scene was a sex game

that the wife really enjoyed. He told the jury, "I didn't rape my wife. How can you rape your wife?" The jury agreed, acquitting the husband. The couple is now separated.

HOT CHOCOLATE

A Santa Ana, California, woman became enraged when her husband, a cancer sufferer, ate a chocolate Easter bunny that she had her eye on. So she allegedly doused him with rubbing alcohol and set him on fire.

3

BOY, IS THAT DUMB

IDIOTIC POLITICIANS, VOLUME 1

After a teen squirt-gun battle escalated into real gunplay that resulted in the death of a 15-year-old boy, Boston Mayor Raymond L. Flynn asked stores to stop selling Super Soaker squirt guns. Evidently, selling handguns, knives, assault rifles, and baseball bats is okay with the mayor, who is determined to save his city's youth by clamping down on the summer's hottest toy. A Boston city councilman used considerable understatement when he commented, "It's a really silly idea to point to a toy as a major force behind urban crime."

IN THE ALL-TIME DUMB IDEA DEPARTMENT . . .

The Super 8 Motel chain, evidently figuring to save a few dollars, set up a credit card reservation program that employed prisoners at the Springfield Correctional Facility in Yankton, South Dakota. Guess what? The prisoners tried to steal credit card numbers, so the program had to be shut down.

YOUR TAX DOLLARS AT WORK

A Los Angeles physician convicted of collecting millions of dollars in fraudulent insurance payments is collecting $256 a month in state disability benefits—because he's stressed out. Evidently, fraud, theft, and tax evasion can take a whole lot out of you.

BUMBLING TOURIST OF THE YEAR

The *African Queen,* the steamboat that had the title role in the famous 1951 movie with Humphrey Bogart and Katharine Hepburn, nearly didn't survive an encounter with a clumsy tourist. The guy was apparently snapping a picture when he somehow stumbled into an electrical switch on the dock, starting the lift that raises the craft from the water each night. Unfortunately, only the bow of the boat was attached. The stern filled with water, nearly dragging the boat under before it was rescued.

OHHHH, AHHH, GRIND THOSE VALVES, BABY . . .

A New Jersey Hyundai dealer sent a recall letter to more than a thousand customers announcing that they could call an 800 number to make an appointment for a mechanic to repair potentially corroding valves on their Excels. But when someone inserted the phone number, he or she typed "900" instead of "800"—which directed the calls to a telephone sex line.

Wonder how many customers decided their valves felt better anyway?

OINK!

A senior vice president of the New York City Transit Authority was home recuperating from a triple-bypass operation when he spoke to 28 of his executives by speaker phone. Evidently anxious to prove his virility when he returned to work, he told the listeners, "Get an auditorium that will fit all the surface managers." When a female executive asked why, he replied, "So you, me, and [another female executive] can have sex onstage."

The next day, the senior vice president lost his $115,000-a-year job—and his replacement was the woman to whom he made the remark.

ADDING INSULT TO INJURY

A 20-year-old Dallas, Texas, man, facing up to 10 years in jail for stamp theft, offered to trade a $7,900 restitution check in return for not having to fulfill his time in jail. There was only one small problem—the $7,900 check was forged. He now faces another 10-year sentence for forgery.

IN THE DUMBEST BUREAUCRATS CATEGORY . . .

Are the winners the Coeur D'Alene, Idaho, authorities who sent undercover detectives to arrest a 70-year-old woman? The charge: selling Avon products from her home, which isn't zoned for commercial business. It seems the woman sold Avon products door-to-door for 46 years, until arthritis forced her to work out of her house. Evidently, the local government would much prefer she go on welfare. And do you believe that no one else in town is selling anything worse than lipstick?

MILITARY INJUSTICE

A 30-year-old sergeant who had been named the Indiana National Guard noncommissioned officer of the year in 1990 was demoted and sentenced to four days in jail for refusing to remove a cap he wore under his helmet. Sounds reasonable until you learn the soldier was wearing the cap under doctor's orders to protect severely burned skin.

WHY DAN QUAYLE CAN'T SPELL "POTATO"

Below are our favorite reasons for the source of Dan Quayle's spelling problems:

* Because he missed the "Sesame Street" episode with the talking vegetables.
  —Rep. Charles Schumer

* Because the person sitting next to him at the bar exam didn't know how to spell it.
  —Democratic pollster Harrison Hickman

* Because there's no golf club called a potato wedge.
  —Democratic strategist Larry Harrington

* Because he figured it was spelled the same way as Idahoe.
  —Schumer, again

IT MUST'VE FLOATED AWAY

No, Gas City, Indiana, isn't Danny's hometown, but as one of the state's more famous native sons, he must have some cosmic influence. Maybe that's why 200 people with shovels, metal detectors, and a backhoe were unable to find a time capsule buried 50 years ago during the town's centennial celebration. Undeterred by this civic black eye, townspeople buried a new time capsule to be dug up 50 years hence. We think a large neon sign on a 25-foot pole is in order.

MONKEY BUSINESS

Animal-rights' activists picketed a Pittsburgh hospital in which a baboon's liver was transplanted into a dying man. Said one, "We don't believe you should sacrifice one species for another. No one asked the baboon what he thought." What we think is that the activists should be the ones to tell a woman that her child or spouse would have to die to save the life of a baboon.

TEXTBOOK EXAMPLE: WHY I SHOULDN'T DRINK

A Pierre, South Dakota, man evidently was filled to the gills with good cheer but was looking for more. So he wandered through the doors of what he thought was another saloon and asked the friendly face behind the bar for a drink. He'd made just one little mistake—the "saloon" was the police station and the guy behind the "bar" was the dispatcher.

THE PRINCIPAL CAUSE OF STUPIDITY

A Dedham, Massachusetts, high school girl wanted to go to the junior prom, but she didn't feel like asking some guy. So she asked a female friend to go with her, then went to the principal to buy tickets. The principal, however, told her that the prom was "couples only," and the only way same-sex couples could attend was if they were gay—because state law prohibits discrimination against homosexuals. In other words, the girl, who is heterosexual, couldn't go to the dance unless she declared herself a lesbian. Fortunately, the absurdity of this rule caused a public outcry that eventually led the principal to cancel the "couples only" policy, so anyone could go.

STRIPPER GETS BURNED

A 24-year-old Buffalo, New York, man would have been better off holding up liquor stores or convenience stores. You see, his attempt to make a few illegal dollars involved stripping copper wire from a transformer at a Niagara Mohawk Power Company substation. Sure enough, he touched the wrong wire and ended up in critical condition with serious burns.

ARRESTING ESSAY

Americans are supposed to be able to say or write anything without fear of retribution. At least that's what must have been in the mind of a Providence, Rhode Island, high school student who wrote an essay describing in detail how his 14-year-old friend shot and killed a 76-year-old store owner. The cops graded the paper $A+$ and arrested the alleged murderer.

MUSEUM EXHIBIT ATTRACTS SWARMS

Attention, lovers of fine art: If you're really lucky, the Fine Art Gallery at the Cheney Cowles Museum in Spokane, Washington, might schedule an encore of last winter's main exhibit—which featured cow skulls and road kill such as dead rabbits and a flattened coyote. During the exhibit, the museum had to call in exterminators to deal with flies, beetles, and other pests that began to feed on the "art." Now, aren't you sorry you missed it?

STUPENDOUS STUPIDITY

A Jacksonville, Florida, couple was arrested after their 3-year-old son shot and killed their 2-year-old daughter with a loaded gun left lying around the house. Police found dozens of other guns in the residence, including three more within easy reach of the children. The couple faces five years in jail—does that seem like enough?

HIS 30-YEAR-OLD DOG WOULDN'T ROLL OVER EITHER

A 79-year-old Key West, Florida, man told police that his roommate was so stubborn that after he fell on the floor, he wouldn't answer him. He complained that the roommate just lay there on the floor ignoring him for two months—until police discovered that the roommate had been dead the whole time. The 79-year-old was sent for a mental exam.

BE CAREFUL WHO YOU NEEDLE

Three teenage girls asked a 27-year-old Muskogee, Oklahoma, man to give them tattoos, and he complied. Then some parents complained, and police arrested the man—not on the misdemeanor charge of tattooing, but on the felony charge of injury to a minor. For doing the girls a favor, he now faces a possible sentence of *life* in prison.

TRANSEXUAL AIRLINES

John Stearns became a pilot for Continental Airlines in 1984 after a 20-year Air Force career that included flying 381 missions in Vietnam. In 1989, he told the airline that he was taking leave to have a series of operations in order to become Jessica Stearns. Continental promptly fired him/her, claiming that Stearns's becoming a woman jeopardized cockpit and flight safety—in other words, women can serve coffee but not fly planes. Stearns sued, and Continental settled, putting her in the driver's seat.

COUNTY EXORCISES SATAN

Some residents of Prescott, Arizona, wondered what "possessed" whoever named a street in a residental development Satan's Arch Drive. So 22 people who live on the street petitioned the County Board of Supervisors to change the name, arguing that the devilish name was scaring away prospective home buyers. So Satan's Arch Drive is now Arch Drive. But we wonder—if the name bothered these 22 people so much, why did they buy homes on that street in the first place?

SAY "CHEESE," STUPID

Two less-than-brilliant Syracuse, New York, men broke into the home of an attorney and were evidently having such a good time that they snapped each other's pictures as they collected loot. The cops later recovered the camera—with the film still inside. The victim had it developed and turned the conclusive evidence over to the police.

NEW JERSEY HAS EGG ON FACE

Diner customers all over the Garden State were in an uproar after the New Jersey State Health Department issued regulations banning restaurants from serving runny or raw eggs. That meant no eggs sunny side up or over easy, not to mention poached eggs in eggs Benedict. The regulation became the subject of national ridicule. And Johnny Carson suggested it was easier to get a gun in New Jersey, than eggs sunny side up. "You can get an Uzi in one day, but there's a two-week waiting period for Caesar salad." Shortly afterward, red-faced officials rescinded the ban.

FLOWERS LAND ANOTHER GUY IN HOT WATER

A Trenton, New Jersey, couple reconciled for a few years after their divorce, then split again. She went to court to get a restraining order preventing him from contacting her. He felt so much remorse that he sent flowers to her as an apology. She called the cops, and a judge sentenced him to two years' probation for violating the restraint order.

ADOLF THE HACKER

Does Microsoft's wildly successful computer software program Windows contain a secret anti-Jewish message? Computer buffs discovered that a print font included with the program had substituted for the letters *NYC* three symbols: a skull and crossbones, a star of David, and a thumbs-up sign. Microsoft denied any knowledge of the alleged message or any intent to imbed a secret message.

ARE THE MOVIE RIGHTS AVAILABLE?

A woman stopped her family van at a highway rest stop in Newport, Tennessee, so her children could go to the bathroom. She took her daughters to the ladies' room while her 5-year-old son headed into the men's room. A few minutes later, she piled the kids back into the van and took off. Seventy miles down the road, she pulled into a fast-food restaurant to order lunch. It was only then that she discovered she'd left her son in Newport.

4

WHAT A WAY
TO GO

GO DIRECTLY TO JAIL, DO NOT PASS GO

A 25-year-old Doylestown, Pennsylvania, man pleaded guilty
to criminal homicide for shooting a friend in the chest with
an arrow after an argument about Monopoly game rules.

IN THE REALLY, REALLY DUMB IDEA DEPARTMENT

A 17-year-old boy was woodchuck hunting with his 31-year-
old friend in a Potter, New York, field when he got the idea it
might be fun to hide and make grunting noises like a woodchuck. You guessed it—the 31-year-old man shot and killed
him.

RUBBED THE WRONG WAY

A 15-year-old Kansas boy who squeezed his friend's head
while giving him a "Dutch rub" faced murder charges. The
reason: The friend died from the rub.

A MONSTER GOT HIM

A "monster" truck veered off the track at a Galesburg, Michigan, speedway, killing a 6-year-old boy. Just a month earlier, another monster truck had killed an 82-year-old spectator in Niagara Falls, New York.

HE BRAGGED, HE CHOKED, HE CROAKED

A 17-year-old Dekalb, Mississippi, boy was sitting in the school cafeteria discussing with his friends who could eat a sandwich the fastest. The 17-year-old decided to win the argument by shoving almost all of a ham sandwich into his mouth. Instead, he ended his life, choking to death.

PLAYING LOBSTER

A 24-year-old employee of the U.S. Fish and Wildlife Service was taking a steam bath with some friends near a volcanic vent in Hawaii Volcanoes National Park. As she got up to leave, she slipped, fell 15 feet down the 2½-foot vent from which the steam was rising and was scalded to death.

DEADLY SEDUCTION

A Vista, California, doctor was arrested on rape and murder charges after he allegedly took a date to a San Diego motel, then knocked her out with chloroform so he could rape her. However, she died, with a lethal dose of chloroform in her body.

A SHOCKING TALE

A 22-year-old Canton, Ohio, man was electrocuted while shaving with his electric razor.

ANGELS WITH CLEAN FACES

A 14-year-old Fox Lake, Illinois, boy died after sniffing the fumes from Scotchguard, an aerosol fabric protectant. Seven of his friends were hospitalized. A spokesperson for 3M, makers of Scotchguard, said the death was the twentieth attributed to the product's misuse over the last two years.

QUICK, GRAB A SHOVEL!

A 25-year-old Virginia man was killed in Hamden, Connecticut, when he lost control of his car, crashed into a cemetery, and was hurled from the car into a headstone. All they had to do was toss on a couple of bouquets.

ANOTHER REASON NOT TO PICK UP YOUR ROOM

A 4-year-old New York City boy who chose a closet as his hiding place for a game of hide-and-seek was crushed to death by the weight of the clothing on his chest.

MOWED DOWN

An 8-year-old girl sitting on the front porch of her grandmother's house in Manchester, Kentucky, was killed by a rock flung from a county highway department mowing machine.

SCENES FROM A MAUL

A 20-year-old college student who was collecting soil samples for a mining company in northeastern Ontario, Canada, was mauled to death by a black bear. No word on whether the bear was against exploitation of mineral rights.

GARTH BROOKS FANS KILL WOMAN

A Tulsa, Oklahoma, man desperately dialing 911 to get help when his wife had a heart attack couldn't get through because the local telephone system was overloaded by fans of country singer Garth Brooks who were calling for concert tickets. By the time the man finally reached the help line, his wife had died.

THE OVERCONFIDENCE AWARD

A Coupeville, Washington, man was drinking with some buddies one Saturday afternoon near the Deception Pass Bridge. The man started bragging that he'd leapt from higher elevations than the 140 feet from the bridge to the water below. And, evidently seeking to impress his friends further, he shouted a cheerful "Yahoo!" and jumped. However, witnesses saw the man's body being sucked into a whirlpool in the rough, 300-foot-deep water. A search failed to turn up his body.

A LITTLE TO THE LEFT—SPLAT!

A Long Island man was working his very first day as a garbage collector when he directed the driver who was backing up the truck. Evidently, the neophyte trashman wasn't too good at hand signals, because the truck ran over him, crushing him to death.

DRUNKEN HORSE RIDING OFTEN FATAL

Evidently, riding a horse while drunk is as dangerous as driving a car while drunk. At least that's the conclusion of a study by the U.S. Centers for Disease Control, which found that the rider was intoxicated in more than half of all fatal horseback-riding accidents studied. Guess the riders figured that they couldn't get into trouble because the horse was sober.

ANOTHER REASON TO HOLD ON TO YOUR BALLS

A Calgary, Canada, man drowned while attempting to retrieve golf balls from a pond on the third hole of a local golf course.

"IT'S A BEAUTIFUL DAY IN THE NEIGHBOR-OOF!"

A 2-year-old Hialeah, Florida, girl was climbing up a dresser to turn on the TV when the set fell, killing her.

SLIMED

A Los Angeles husband and his nine-months-pregnant wife were sleeping in their bed when a river of mud poured in through their open window and suffocated them. The mud flow was caused by days of torrential rains.

ACCIDENT OR DIVINE RETRIBUTION

A 16-year-old Roxboro, North Carolina, boy was awaiting trial on charges that he killed a motorist by throwing a 60-

pound boulder off a highway bridge. He took a job at a manufacturing plant to help pay for his defense. Shortly afterward, he died by electrocution while working on the plant's roof.

BLACK DEATH

A man hopped a coal train heading east out of Denver, then fell asleep in a coal car as the train moved across the plains. Unfortunately, he didn't wake up when the train arrived to dump its load in Holcomb, Kansas. The sleeping man was killed as the car was dumped into a 25-foot-deep coal pit and 300 tons of coal landed on top of him.

BELIEVE THE WARNINGS

Many plastic and cellophane items carry a warning about the dangers of suffocation. But something like an Easter basket seems so harmless it's easy to forget that it's wrapped in cellophane. A 3-year-old Long Island, girl hid some of that wrapping underneath her bed covers, rolled over onto it during the night, and died.

YOUR MOTHER *WAS* RIGHT!

Two boys playing pirate were dueling with curtain rods on a Queens, New York, street when one boy slipped, impaling the other boy's head with his rod.

LIFE STINKS, THEN YOU DIE

A 16-year-old boy who killed himself with his father's gun may have committed suicide because his parents refused to let him bathe since his baby sister had drowned in a bathtub 15 years before. The principal of the boy's school said students often ridiculed him because of his body odor.

5

AMONG THE
THINGS YOU DIDN'T
WANT TO KNOW

THE REPUBLICAN PLAN TO SOLVE HUNGER IN AMERICA?

A Garden City, California, couple, Linda and Dave Dunlap, produced a video entitled *The Fine Art of Dumpster Dining*, which they distributed free to shelters and other agencies dealing with the homeless. Their aim was to teach the homeless to avoid poisoning when scavenging for food out of trash bins. Sounds like a noble idea, but we hope the Bush Administration hasn't heard about it—they'd probably want to substitute the video and dumpster dining for the Food Stamp program.

DANNY'S DING DONG ON DISPLAY

The ultimate gift for Quayle watchers went on the market last year when Patagonia Trading Co. manufactured a limited-edition "anatomically correct" Dan Quayle doll. Patagonia became famous two years ago when Danny thoroughly embarrassed his wife and entourage by purchasing one of its anatomically correct South American Indian dolls while on a state visit to Chile. Wonder who provided the "inside" information for the Danny doll design?

IS THIS WHY OPPOSITES ATTRACT?

A researcher at the California Institute of Technology has discovered microscopic magnetic crystals in human brain tissue. Other species use such crystals as an internal compass to help them navigate, so it's possible people who have a good sense of direction are people who make the best use of their magnetism. It also may explain why so many of us are irresistibly attracted to the refrigerator.

I'D LIKE A MILLION DOLLARS, PLEASE

In Sante Fe, New Mexico, a 22-year-old unmarried woman on public assistance gave birth to quadruplets after taking fertility drugs. Care of the children, which must be paid by Medicaid, could reach $1 million. State authorities were besieged with telephone calls from angry taxpayers wondering why they would have to pick up the tab when a young single woman on welfare decided to take fertility drugs.

CAKE WALKING

Researchers at the University of Colorado discovered that some unsuccessful dieters unconsciously sabotage their weight-loss programs by sleepwalking into the kitchen to gorge themselves in the middle of the night. Scientists found

these people ate huge amounts of food, some of it bizarre—
including cat food and buttered cigarettes.

THE ULTIMATE NIGHTMARE

Stories of computer viruses have terrified computer users,
but none more than the newest disease—the Barry Manilow
Virus. This covert program infiltrates even the most sophisti-
cated systems and forces the machines to endlessly play
Manilow's greatest hits, including "Looks Like We Made It,"
"I Write the Songs," and "Copacabana."

THE RIGHT TO BARE ARMS—AND LEGS, AND . . .

When more than 150 church members in tiny Crosby, North
Dakota (pop. 1312), signed a petition to ban striptease dancing, the rest of the town rallied behind the owner of Jerry's
Lounge. The local bar imported strippers from Minneapolis
to perform every Tuesday, Wednesday, and Thursday night,
attracting big spenders from across the border in Canada.
The issue went to a town vote, and the right to bare tri-
umphed 342 to 190. The turnout was 20 percent higher than
in the recent mayoral election.

$10 MILLION PEEP

A couple sleeping in a room at a Holiday Inn in Moncks
Corner, South Dakota, awoke in the middle of the night to see
a narrow beam of light that seemed to be shining from the
center of a wall mirror. A subsequent investigation by the
local sheriff's department revealed that someone had drilled
more than 100 peepholes through walls in the 172-room
establishment, then scraped the backing off the mirrors to

provide a view. The couple and the rock band of which they were members sued the Holiday Inn for invasion of privacy and were awarded a whopping $10.1 million. The culprit was never found.

BON APPÉTIT!

A Long Island, New York, duck farm that supplied duck livers for the foie gras served in many of New York's most prestigious restaurants was raided by the Suffolk County District Attorney's office and charged with animal abuse. According to authorities, the farm shoved a foot-long metal tube down the ducks' throats three times a day and force-fed the birds huge amounts of food using compressed air. Frequently, too much food caused the ducks to explode. Employees were awarded a bonus if they blew up fewer than 50 ducks per month. Many ducks got so fat that they were unable to walk, and the tops of their bills were cut off so they couldn't eat or drink normally.

THE WORLD'S MOST BORING CAT HOUSE

The Tangent, Oregon, City Council has been evicted from its meeting place by its landlord—which happens to be a cat. The governing body of this city had been meeting in a house willed to a feline named Kitty Cat by its owner, who died at age 82 in 1983. John Bass had left the house and a $100,000 estate to care for the cat. Because the city will inherit the house when Kitty dies, the cat's lawyer allowed the Council to use the house for meetings. However, when the council members refused to share the $5,000 cost of a new furnace, the cat (through its lawyer) said scat.

PUSH! PUSH! FOR HEAVEN'S SAKE, BREATHE *OUT!*

No, this isn't the title of a new film from Troma Studios, the folks who've brought us such classics as *Barbarian Nymphs From Hell.* It's a recent discovery by archaeologists, whose examination of 1,600-year-old remains led to the conclusion that women in the Middle East ate hashish to ease the pain of childbirth. We don't know about you, but we're *shocked.*

DAM! BEAVER OPERATION BRINGS BLUSHES

Wildlife experts in Denver, Colorado, called a news conference to demonstrate the first operation to implant a birth-control device in a beaver. Apparently, a beaver population explosion has been causing turmoil in Denver suburbs. Anyway, the television cameras were rolling until embarrassed experts stopped the procedure, explaining sheepishly that the beaver undergoing the implant turned out to be . . . a male.

WILL MADD TURN INTO MADS?

For the first time in recent history, two states—Texas and Louisiana—reported more deaths from firearms than from motor-vehicle accidents. Experts predict more states will soon join the ranks. Anyone for a campaign against drunken shooting? Maybe a designated triggerman? Tune in.

$1.6 MILLION FOR DRINKING ON THE JOB

A Fort Lauderdale, Florida, woman who had worked as a nude dancer was awarded $1.6 million after successfully arguing that the automobile crash that made her a quadriplegic was caused by the fact that she had to drink on the job.

Although Florida law normally bans providing workers compensation in cases of drunkenness, the woman's attorney proved that part of her job was to encourage club patrons to buy her champagne.

SWALLOWS NIX TRADITION, TURN CHIC

For the first time in memory, not a single swallow was spotted returning to the mission at San Juan Capistrano as the traditional bells rang on March 19. Instead, observers spotted a flock of the birds in trendy Malibu. Have the birds given up monk-watching for the babes on the beach?

LEGAL BRIEFS

A man issued a $35 speeding ticket in Drummon, Montana, was so enraged that he showed up in court to pay his fine with a check written on a pair of tattered underwear. The judge took the briefs to the bank, which cashed them. Then he docked the speeder a whopping $110 for contempt of court.

SYMPATHY WITH THE DEVIL

We sympathize with any substitute teacher who has to cope with rowdy junior high school kids. But an Irvington, New Jersey, substitute may have gone a shade too far when she allegedly chanted voodoo curses and sprinkled potions on her seventh-graders to get them to behave. According to school authorities, the voodoo teacher threw a chair at the kids, then warned them that she would curse them and burn down their houses if they weren't quiet. At least she didn't sacrifice a chicken. On the other hand . . .

PASS THE TOFU, PLEASE

You may want to give vegetarianism a try after reading a report on meat inspection prepared by investigators for the U.S. Department of Agriculture. The report revealed that the USDA's normal inspection procedures are so sloppy that meat labeled "USDA Prime" and "USDA Choice" contained everything from pigs' ears to feet and tails. Last year, the USDA inspected just 694 out of 200,000 retailers. Bon appétit!

DEATH ON THE HIGHWAY

Before you decide to play games with that semi roaring up behind you, you might want to take a moment to consider the findings of a study conducted by the National Transportation Safety Board. More than half of all trucks stopped at random in a five-state survey failed a brake test.

DOES IT COME BY THE CASE?

Forget about moonlight and perfume—what really turns a man on is nitric oxide. Scientists at Johns Hopkins University determined that penile erection is triggered by minute amounts of nitric oxide, a chemical generated by nerves. The findings led to speculation that a cream containing nitric oxide could be the solution for male sexual problems, from impotence to excessive erection.

AN ITSY-BITSY, TEENY-WEENY YELLOW POLKA DOT—CONDOM?

The newest thing in birth control, hatched in the mind of a Cranbury, New Jersey, surgeon, is a beige latex bikini bottom with a condom in the crotch. A woman slips it on, and, presto, is protected against AIDS and pregnancy with less risk than the standard male condom. The invention still needs some testing before it gets FDA approval. Any volunteers?

HUMONGOUS FUNGUS

The Washington State Department of Natural Resources has announced the discovery of what may be the world's largest single organism—a giant fungus that covers two and a half square miles. The fungus, which grows underground and kills trees at their roots, may be a thousand years old. Do you know what's lurking under your yard?

OUR EDUCATION SYSTEM AT WORK

A 1992 report by the U.S. Census Bureau showed that 34.8 percent of high school–aged American children had dropped out of school or had been left back. That's up from 29.1 percent in 1980. Aren't you proud?

"SMOKED" TUNA

An Ardsley, New York, mother opened a can of Bumble Bee tuna to make lunch for her 5-year-old daughter. She was about to mix in some mayonnaise when she saw a funny-looking black spot in the tuna. Turns out it was funny stuff indeed—a partially smoked marijuana cigarette.

THE ICE AGE COMETH

The dust and smoke circulating in the atmosphere from the 1991 volcanic eruption of Mount Pinatubo in the Philippines cooled the entire Northern Hemisphere about 1.5 degrees in 1992. Imagine the impact of all the hot air from the 1992 Presidential elections?

THE BREAST STROKE LEGAL IN ARIZONA

Charges against a male Arizona high school teacher who fondled a 16-year-old girl were dismissed—because such sexual behavior isn't illegal in the state unless physical force is used. Outraged citizens formed a campaign to lobby the state legislature to change the law.

I KNEW DOOGIE HOWSER, AND MARVIN, YOU'RE *NO* DOOGIE HOWSER

Marvin Lee of Duncan, Oklahoma, skipped high school to go to the University of Oklahoma at age 13. Four years later, he graduated Phi Beta Kappa. So what did this genius decide to do? He went back to his hometown to enroll in high school to get his high school diploma. The reason: He didn't want to go on to medical school without experiencing some of those highlights of youth such as going to a prom and trying out for the basketball team.

MALE TAX?

In her book *Men Are Not Cost-Effective*, a Stanford University psychologist points out that most of the nation's prison cells—94 percent of those in California, for example—are filled with men. Her conclusion: Men cost society so much extra money that they should pay extra taxes as a "user fee" for tying up so much money in the criminal justice system.

The male counter-argument: Tax women because they're the ones who have babies we have to educate.

YOUR TAX DOLLARS AT WORK

The idiotic workers who were sent to a Boston park to paint and fill a long-neglected wading pool were allegedly too lazy to sweep up broken glass covering the bottom of the pool before they readied it for use. The result: 18 children cut their feet before authorities closed the pool again.

HOW TO GET THE ATTENTION OF CITY HALL

A Troy, Illinois, construction crew found an extremely effective way to get the full attention of civic officials. While using a crane to demolish a burned-out bakery, they inadvertently knocked a huge hole in the City Hall office of the city administrator. The administrator remarked, "We have an open-door policy. But this is carrying it a little too far."

SLIMY MAYOR OF THE YEAR AWARD

Spartanburg, South Carolina, is one of 700 communities nationwide that proclaimed a Days of Remembrance week for six million Jews killed in the Holocaust. The mayor, however, argued against publicizing the event, saying that it might offend German automaker BMW, which is eyeing the city as a possible site for a $1 billion plant. Local Jewish leaders called the suggestion "outrageous." A BMW spokesman added, "Equating anything that a German company does with the horrors of Nazi Germany is irrelevant."

GOOD NEWS ABOUT MICHAEL JACKSON!

In a book published by the Smithsonian Institution, college professor Jib Fowles reported a study showing that, on the average, the life span of a celebrity was 13 years shorter than that of the average American. Female celebrities died an average of 22 years younger than the average woman, while male celebrities kicked the bucket 8 years earlier. The primary reasons for the early deaths are accidents and suicide. Extensive travel and substance abuse are the primary causes of the higher accident rate.

THE HIGH KITER'S LIST

In case you missed it, the five Congressmen below are the only members of the exclusive $300,000 Club—in other words, they wrote bad checks for more than that astonishing figure. They are:

- Stephen Solarz (D., N.Y.), $594,646 on 743 checks
- Carl Perkins (D., Ky.), $565,651 on 514 checks
- Harold Ford (D., Tenn.), $552,447 on 388 checks
- Robert Mrazek (D., N.Y.), $351,609 on 920 checks
- Robert Davis (R., Mich.), $344,450 on 878 checks

HOSE DOWN SAND—TO SAVE IT

Dauphin Island, Alabama, like a lot of barrier beach areas in the U.S., is rapidly losing sand. So one resident came up with a new idea to save it: collect tens of thousands of pairs of used panty hose for divers to anchor below water in order to trap the sand. Unfortunately, the U.S. Army Corps of Engineers is skeptical. But the dedicated man has collected 500 pairs of panty hose anyway—sounds like a good hobby.

SPOILSPORT

In 1934, a group of 37 World War I vets purchased a bottle of 1917 Hennessy Five-Star Cognac and decided that the bottle would remain unopened until only one of them was left alive. Well, in 1992, 92-year-old Chester Chastek of Lacey, Washington, became that last man. But there's one problem—Chastek doesn't drink and won't start, no matter what the pledge. So we wrote him and volunteered to be surrogate cognac drinkers—noble, huh?

OH, DO IT TO ME, SKIPPER, DO IT TO ME!

Tens of thousands of viewers, many of them children, were startled one afternoon shortly after 5:30 when a soundtrack from a hard-core pornographic movie popped up in the middle of an episode of "Gilligan's Island." A girl's very explicit description of what a man was doing to her aired for about three minutes before the station pulled it off the air.

DOES IT GO WITH A WHOPPER?

A Canadian affiliate of McDonald's Corp. went to court to stop a Montreal sex shop from offering contraceptives labeled McCondoms. The restaurant chain argued that McCondoms violated its trademark McLanguage and that the logo on the rubbers, a stylized letter *M* in yellow print, is an illegal copy of its registered golden arches.

A $177,000 SLAP

A Tallahassee, Florida, prison guard got angry when an inmate spit on him, so he slapped the convict. Naturally, in this day and age, the convict sued. The result for Florida taxpayers: A $10,000 award to the convict, $37,000 to his lawyers, and $130,000 to lawyers for the state of Florida. The total: $177,000 for a slap.

TITANIC ATTITUDE STINKS

Would you give your seat on a lifeboat to a person of the opposite sex who was not a spouse or a child? According to a survey conducted by the *Pittsburgh Post-Gazette*, only 35 percent of men believe in the old adage "Women and children first." Women believe in it, however—only 3 percent would give up their seats to a man. By the way, in a result that says as much about marriage as it does about chivalry, one-third of the men and 60 percent of the women wouldn't give up the seat for their spouse, either.

SHOCKING STATISTIC

Anyone who thinks all the recent attention to the problem of sexual harassment isn't justified should be told this one statistic: A study conducted by the National Institute on Drug Abuse discovered that 12 million American women had been raped at least once.

6

IF YOU THINK YOU'VE GOT TROUBLE

PAMPERING THE BABY . . .

A Southfield, Minnesota, 2-year-old tumbled out of a ninth-floor apartment window and was falling to certain death 80 feet below when his diaper snagged on a bush, stopping his descent. The diaper tape finally gave way, and the infant fell a few feet to the ground, naked but virtually unhurt. We bet his new nickname is Lucky.

SAVED BY THE SKIN OF HIS TEETH

A Denver, Colorado, cab driver was shot in the mouth during a robbery—and walked out of the hospital that night. What was the reason for this miracle? The bullet hit the man's dentures and fragmented, causing only minor cuts.

MAN HOOKED BY FISH

Most fish stories center around the one that got away. But in the case of a 31-year-old Evansville, Indiana, fisherman, the story is about the fish that hooked him. He had hauled in a 5-pound catfish and tossed it to a friend. The friend threw the catfish back at the fisherman, and the momentum of the toss caused a 5-inch bony fin to puncture the fisherman's lung. The impaled angler was rushed to the hospital for emergency surgery. Unfortunately, the catfish didn't survive to brag to his fellow fish—it was filleted and frozen.

TARDY TURTLE

Runaway pets usually turn up in a few days. But in the case of Myrtle the Turtle, a 45-year-old desert tortoise who moves very slowly, the process of recovery took a lot longer. Myrtle, who evidently had a yen for rambling, ran away from her Long Beach, California, owner in 1982. She was on the lam for 10 years before she was spotted strolling down the sidewalk—nearly 200 miles from home. Because desert tortoises are a threatened species, Myrtle had been registered with the state's Department of Fish and Game and wore a numbered tag, which allowed authorities to return her to her owner. But she was mum on how she'd spent her time on her little stroll.

IN THE BAD-LUCK DEPARTMENT

In each of the last two elections, Allen Olejniczak ran for alderman in Thorp, Wisconsin. In each of the last two elections, Olejniczak and his opponent tied, each getting the exact same number of votes. In 1990, he lost a coin flip that decided the contest; in 1992, his opponent's name was drawn out of a hat. The two-time loser's comment: "I hope I never go to Las Vegas, with my luck."

WORKERS ARRIVE HOME PICKLED

Several workers in a New York City mustard factory were in a pickle when a 20,000-gallon tank ruptured, flooding them with vinegar. At least 10 employees were treated for nausea and breathing problems caused by the accident that left a block of Manhattan's Upper East Side smelling like a tossed salad. Firefighters doused the site with a gigantic dose of bicarbonate of soda.

LONDON BRIDGE ISH FALLIN' DOWN

The old rhyme finally proved true when a 52-year-old man crashed into London Bridge, partially toppling the structure. Of course, the world's most famous bridge no longer resides in England, but in the Arizona resort town of Lake Havasu City, where it is Arizona's second most popular tourist attraction. The driver, who pled guilty to drunken-driving charges, was ordered to pay for damages that could top $50,000.

WOULD-BE SUICIDE GETS AN *A* FOR EFFORT, BUT . . .

Ever have those days when nothing goes right, no matter how hard you try? A 30-year-old Kenmore, New York, man evidently did when he decided to kill himself by leaping out of a fourth-story window. Because the building's windows don't open, the man took a running leap, smashed through the glass, fell 40 feet, and landed on the top of a car that absorbed most of the impact. A little dazed but undaunted, the would-be suicide jumped up, ran into the building, took the elevator to the fourth floor, leaped out the window again—and landed on the same car. This time he broke his wrist and ankle, so police caught up with him and took him to the hospital before he could try a third time.

DUNNING THE DEAD

A Tulsa, Oklahoma, widow filed a $40 million lawsuit against a Texas evangelist, saying that he continued to send solicitation letters to her dead husband promising that God would restore his health. The evangelist was already under investigation by the Texas attorney general's office after information surfaced that he promised to personally pray for people who sent in contributions, but in fact had hired a mail-processing company that cashed the checks and tossed away the prayer requests.

THE DOG ATE MY HOMEWORK, VERSION 2

A 49-year-old West Palm Beach, Florida, woman was arrested when undercover cops posing as house hunters found several marijuana plants growing in pots on her back porch. The woman's defense: The illegal plants were the only food her pet iguana, Kiko, would eat. After the plants were taken away, the lizard went on a hunger strike and died. Then prosecuters dropped the charges because they determined that the police search had been illegal.

WITCHES' WRATH

Being "politically correct" may mean chucking some children's stories. At least that's the aim of two women who described themselves as witches. The two requested that the

Mount Diablo, California, school system ban the children's story *Hansel and Gretel* because it "teaches that it is all right to burn witches and steal their property." Added the high priestess of the local coven, "Witches don't eat children and we don't have long noses." No word about a possible boycott of *The Wizard of Oz*.

OWWW!

A group of balding men filed a federal lawsuit against a New Jersey hair-replacement company. The reason: The company's technique consisted of sewing a bad wig to the scalp. Said their attorney, "They looked like they'd been wearing a crown of thorns." The process allegedly caused constant pain and left the men with ugly scars.

IF YOU THINK YOU'VE GOT BAD LUCK . . .

Two Evansville, Indiana, men could have checked into any one of dozens of hotels and been assigned to rooms on any of several floors in each when they decided to spend a night partying and smoking marijuana. But they just happened to end up on the same floor of the same motel as 53 federal narcotics agents who were attending a drug-fighting seminar. No sooner had the two lit up than they were surrounded by enough lawmen to topple a Colombian drug cartel.

A REAL SNAKE IN THE DASH

A woman rented a car from Avis in Melbourne, Florida, and drove almost 2,000 miles to her parents' home near Rochester, New York. As she stopped the car, a four-and-a-half-foot python slithered out from under the dash and wrapped itself around the steering wheel. Turns out the snake had been left in the car by the previous renter. We'd like to know this: How absentminded do you have to be to forget a four-and-a-half-foot python?

BEAUTY IS IN THE EYES OF THE BEHOLDER

Themis Klotz calls the artwork that adorns her front yard *The Monument to Humanity No One Will Be Left to Build After George Bush Has His Winnable Limited Protracted Nuclear War With 20 Million American Acceptable Losses.* To her neighbors, it's a Pontiac station wagon buried under 44 tons of sand interlaced with orange snow fencing and a dolphin-print T-shirt. Nearby are moldy books, lawn chairs, a rusty gas tank, a spare tire, a pencil, a Christmas tree, and a Ben & Jerry's Rainforest Crunch ice cream carton. The town took the case to a jury, which ruled that Ms. Klotz's front yard violated health and fire codes. She's appealing.

LOOK BEFORE YOU LEAP

Someone had swiped the NO DIVING sign from a pier at New York's Coney Island park. So two brothers, ages 26 and 27, walked out on the structure and dove—into just five feet of water. Both hit their heads on the bottom and both were taken to the hospital, paralyzed from the neck down.

DOUBLE "I DO"S GET HER INTO DOO-DOO

A Mississippi woman couldn't decide between two men, so she married both of them—in ceremonies just two days apart. She later admitted the bigamy in court. When the judge asked her which man she wanted, she replied, "Neither one. I'm too young to be married."

THE BAD BOSS AWARDS

The Women's Alliance for Job Equity launched a search for the year's worst boss, a dubious honor. The winners, announced on National Secretary's Week, were:

- 1st Prize: A clerk at a food-distribution center whose duties included going to the boss's apartment early every morning, entering the bedroom, and shaking him and his wife until they awakened.

- 2nd Prize: An executive who walked into the office, plunked the bloody head of a rabid fox on his secretary's desk, and told her to put it in the refrigerator until he could have it tested.

- 3rd Prize: The boss who made his legal secretary bandage his broken toes and examine his mouth for sores.

- "Dishonorable Mention": A boss who made his secretary take dictation while he sat on the john with the bathroom door open.

SCORES DYED IN CONNECTICUT BANK BLAST

No, it's not a misspelling. The incident occurred in a New Haven, Connecticut, bank after packages of bills rigged with dye to deter robberies spontaneously exploded, filling the bank with dye and tear gas.

NO BUTTS IN VERMONT PRISONS

Despite a study that showed 75 percent of prisoners smoked, Vermont decided to ban smoking in all of its prisons and jails. The decision was made for health reasons—but guess who ended up with the world's crankiest prisoners?

7

SCANDAL AROUND
THE WORLD

CALABRIA, ITALY: WOMAN PREGNANT AND HAPPY—
AT AGE 62

A 62-year-old housewife became pregnant after a test-tube conception. A gynecologist implanted a 30-year-old woman's egg that had been fertilized by sperm from the housewife's husband. No word on why a 62-year-old woman would want to become a mother.

CAIRO, EGYPT: THE AYATOLLAH KHOMEINIE
SENSE-OF-HUMOR AWARD

This award goes to our fun-loving friends in the Islamic Jihad, who gunned down Farag Fouda, a Cairo professor and newspaper columnist. The reason: Fouda had made fun of the Jihad's refusal to eat eggplant and squash because the vegetables looked like phallic symbols. Imagine how long Jay Leno would last on Arabic TV.

TOKYO, JAPAN: LAND OF THE RISING SON

Evidently, many Japanese businessmen are so busy trying to conquer the world economically that they can't spare even a few hours once a year to visit an aging parent. So, presto, a company called Japan Efficiency Headquarters stepped in with a wildly popular new service. For $1,200, the company arranges for a whole crew of actors, including infants, to stage a family reunion at which the crew pretends to be children and grandchildren of the lonely seniors. Said the president of the company, "We fill a hole in the heart."

PARIS, FRANCE: LET'S HAVE A BIG HAND FOR . . .

Alexandre, the Parisian hairdresser to the stars, had been inspired in his career by the late Antoine, hairdresser to Claudette Colbert and Josephine Baker. Evidently, there had been a hole in Alexandre's life since Antoine died in 1976. So this year he traveled to the late coiffeur's grave in Poland and exhumed his mentor's right hand, which now sits in a box in Alexandre's apartment, where it gives him great pleasure. In the fall, the hand will make a guest appearance at a mass for Antoine. Now, isn't that special?

SYDNEY, AUSTRALIA: RESCUE, 0-0-0?

An Australian who had evidently been watching the American TV show "Rescue 911" frantically dialed that number for ten minutes when a terrible fire broke out in a business building. There was only one slight problem: In Australia, the emergency number is 000. By the time someone else called the right number, the building was gutted.

JOHANNESBURG, SOUTH AFRICA: SUPERMAN KILLS DAD

A 4-year-old boy dressed up in a Superman costume found a revolver lying around the house. So he decided to emulate his hero by marching into his parents' bedroom, pointing the revolver at his father, shouting, "Papa, you're under arrest," and pulling the trigger. Dad, who wasn't invincible, died.

JERUSALEM, ISRAEL: IF THE SHOE FITS, SPIT

A wedding crisis occurred when the rabbinical court lost the ceremonial shoe used for the ceremony that enables childless widows to remarry. Jewish law mandates that the brother of the dead husband must marry the widow to give her children. To get out of the obligation, the widow must remove a special knee-high shoe from the brother's foot in a rabbi's presence, then spit in it. The problem developed when one brother refused to give back the shoe. Making a new one took more than a month, delaying weddings.

STOCKHOLM, SWEDEN: ALMOST TOO BIZARRE TO BELIEVE

Most of us have snoopy neighbors who notice everything we do. But an 84-year-old Stockholm woman evidently had the least curious neighbors in the world. The woman had apparently donned a coat and hat to sit on her balcony to watch fireworks on New Year's Eve when she slumped forward and died. Then her body remained in the same position on the balcony for two and a half months before anyone noticed.

SAINTES, FRANCE: WHAT PRICE LOVE

A court in this western French town finally settled an age-old question by putting a price tag on intimate marital relations.

It set the value of sex between husband and wife at exactly $54. The ruling came in a case brought by a man whose marital relations were interrupted when a doctor mistakenly daubed his penis with acetic acid. The man missed 10 rendez-vouses with his wife, so the court awarded him $540.

BOGOTA, COLOMBIA: HOMELESS KILLED FOR THEIR CORPSES

As if Colombia didn't have enough problems with drug-related violence, authorities broke up a ring that may have beaten to death as many as 22 homeless people in order to sell the corpses to a university medical school.

DALECARLIA, SWEDEN: LET YOUR FINGERS DO THE WALKING

Some residents of this central Swedish area were up in arms when the telephone company published a directory featuring a painting of a naked woman sporting with a satyr. After receiving 7,500 protests, the phone company mailed out a white adhesive overlay to veil the cover. "People can draw their own pictures," said a company spokesman.

ROME, ITALY: YOU IN THE SHORT PANTS—FREEZE!

Concerned because stores were evading sales taxes by not ringing up purchases and not giving receipts to customers, Italy enacted a law penalizing the practice. But enforcement may have been a little overzealous. A 7-year-old boy walked into a store, put a few liras on the counter to purchase a bag of cheese puffs, and walked out without his receipt. The cops promptly gave him a ticket, and whacked the store with the equivalent of a $300 fine. Italy's finance minister chided the police, but a few days later, a woman got a similar ticket after leaving money on the counter when her 3-year-old grabbed a piece of candy. This occurred, by the way, in a country where organized crime is completely out of control.

MOSCOW, RUSSIA: HITLER'S TEETH SITTING IN RUSSIA'S MILITARY ARCHIVES

A noted historian told a Moscow newspaper that the teeth and dental work of Adolf Hitler and his wife, Eva Braun, are in Russian military archives. He added that the rest of the remains of the Nazi dictator and his bride were destroyed in 1970. The historian offered absolutely no reason why they saved the teeth.

ZINDER, NIGER: SHOW SOME THIGH, NO RAIN FALL FROM SKY

A woman in a miniskirt may make some men's mouths go dry. But in Niger, self-proclaimed Moslem holy men charged that "indecent" clothing worn by women was the cause of the drought afflicting the country. Police had to impose a curfew after the charges instigated riots in the streets.

MADRID, SPAIN: EL TORO BECOMES EL TAME-O

The Spanish bullfight business is booming, with more than 15,000 bullfighting programs generating more than $1 billion in revenue. But critics charge that most of the bulls used today are bred to be weak-legged, timid creatures more afraid of the matadors than the matadors are of them. Charges also surfaced that some bulls are drugged before fights to make them even more placid. Gee, bullfighting is starting to sound like major-league baseball.

HONG KONG: ASIAN GANGS TURNING WEENIES

Hong Kong's triad gangs are reputed to be the toughest in the world, but fear of AIDS is melting even their backbones. The fear has apparently affected the traditional ceremony for inducting new recruits. For centuries, each new member mixed some of his blood in a communal bowl, then all the members of the gang drank from it. Now drinking the mixed blood is out. Instead, the suck blood from their own fingers. Bunch of wimps, we say.

MONTERREY, MEXICO: BURNING WATER

Residents of this Mexican area had been unsuccessfully trying for years to convince authorities that gasoline from a local refinery was seeping into the water supply. Finally, they came up with a convincing demonstration—they drew some water from the tap, tossed in a match, and the water exploded in flame. They got their investigation.

STOCKHOLM, SWEDEN: SOLVING CRIME IS CHILD'S PLAY

Police had combed an area for days looking for a weapon that was key evidence in a case of attempted murder. Then a 7-year-old boy who wants to be a policeman when he grows up began his search near his day-care center. A little while later, he found a knife in a garden—the weapon that led to the conviction. Police gave the boy a cake and a toy patrol car as a reward.

TOKYO, JAPAN: BOY, IS MY TEACHER STRICT!

Ten teachers at a Japanese school for autistic and troubled youth were given suspended sentences and a slap on the wrist, despite having been indicted on forty-four charges for incidents that led to the deaths of four students. Two of the students died from shock after they were beaten with bamboo swords and oars and then thrown into the sea by the teachers. Two others died in escape attempts.

HUIXQUIUCAN, MEXICO: CRIMINAL CROONING

Serenading your lover is a time-honored Mexican tradition. But the less romantic citizens in this suburb of Mexico City got so tired of being awakened in the middle of the night by crooning, love-sick troubadors that they persuaded town authorities to make the practice a criminal offense. In Huixquiucan, you now either keep your love silent or spend 36 hours in the slammer.

JOHANNESBURG, SOUTH AFRICA: A REALLY WICKED WITCHCRAFT

A 2-year-old boy was found in a field outside this city, hideously mutilated in an apparent witchcraft ceremony. Because some witchdoctors believe that children's body parts are necessary for some potions to ward off evil spirits, this toddler had to suffer the horror of having his penis, his testicles, and his thumbs cut off. Due to the damage to his sexual organs, doctors performed a sex-change operation so that he would be raised as a girl.

COLOMBO, SRI LANKA: CONDOM CONVICTION

Safe-sex advocates are preaching the use of condoms around the world. But if you get caught carrying one in this rather prudish country, you could end up in the slammer. It seems that police in Sri Lanka consider carrying a condom evidence of intent to commit a sexual crime.

ANTANANARIVO, MADAGASCAR: HOW TO BEAT A COUP—IGNORE IT

One day in July, a group of soldiers in this Indian Ocean country decided to take over the government, so they grabbed their weapons and seized the government-operated radio station. The government's response: They totally ignored the coup. Guards let the rebels walk in and the army stayed in its barracks. One rebel declared himself leader and broadcast threats and charges against the government for a few hours. When all the commotion didn't produce a response by anyone, the rebels just packed up and slinked away.

ROSTOV-ON-DON, RUSSIA: BEAST OF RUSSIA

A 56-year-old former schoolteacher confessed to raping, slaying, and partially cannibalizing 21 boys, 14 girls, and 18 young women since 1978 in what may have been Russia's worst case of serial murder. The man, a member of the Communist Party and married with a family, often gouged out his victims' eyes; cut off fingers, breasts, and genitals; and ate some flesh. Authorities admitted that they had previously executed the wrong man for some of these murders.

LONDON, ENGLAND: THE UNLUCKIEST MAN OF 1992

A 48-year-old man was paralyzed by polio he contracted when changing the diaper of his infant niece, who had just been immunized against the disease. In very rare cases, the weakened virus used in the vaccine can revert to the potent form and cause the disease in unvaccinated people.

CAIRO, EGYPT: OOPS!

Many Egyptians turn to traditional folk medicine instead of modern medicine, and that has cost a 3-year-old girl her life in a horrible accident. The girl had a throat ailment, which superstition said could be cured by a butcher passing the blunt edge of his cleaver along the afflicted person's throat. The problem was, the butcher made a mistake—he used the sharp edge, which cut the girl's throat. The butcher was sentenced to a year in jail.

KENMARE, IRELAND: BERTHA'S BIRTHDAY BASH

In case you missed it, Bertha, the world's oldest and most prolific cow, turned 48 this year. The grand dame of bovines, who has birthed 39 calves, celebrated with a pail of apples and a few drops of whiskey. The ceremony was broadcast live all across the nation on a popular talk show—which demonstrates how much there is to do in Ireland.

8

THE MOST BIZARRE
SCANDALS OF 1992

BABYSITTER OF THE YEAR

A 27-year-old Houston woman was arrested after the 11-month-old baby she was sitting for died. The reason for the tot's demise: The sitter allegedly stuffed paper towels down his throat to keep him from crying.

FETUS WAS SUPER-SHIELD

A woman who was nine months pregnant was returning to her Compton, California, apartment during the Los Angeles riots when she was shot in the abdomen. She was rushed to the hospital, where doctors delivered a 6-pound, 12-ounce baby girl—with a bullet lodged in her tiny arm. The baby, named Jessica, saved her mother's life by stopping the bullet and, miraculously, survived herself.

DIRTY DOCTOR DOODLES

A surgeon who served as chief of staff at one of the nation's most famous burn hospitals was brought up for disciplinary action by the American College of Surgeons for using a surgical marker to draw pictures on various body parts of his patients. The doodling doc allegedly put happy faces on the penises of two patients and on the upper abdomen of a third. He had previously been suspended by the hospital for a week for placing his initials on the skull of a severely burned 9-month-old infant.

GRANDPA'S IN A CONDOM . . .

You've heard of shotgun weddings, but we'll bet you don't know that a Des Moines, Iowa, man has come up with the shotgun funeral. Specifically, he believes it's a shame for the ashes of people who loved hunting to end up in a cold urn on some mantel. So for the cost of a normal internment, he loads the hunter's ashes into shotgun shells and drives to the hunter's favorite woods, marsh, or other location. After performing whatever ritual the family requests, he loads the shells and blasts away the ashes.

While the shotgun funerals are the man's most popular type of service, he will also put ashes in bowling balls, baseball bats, or almost anything else the departed loved to do. One woman sent her father's ashes to be stuffed into her golf clubs.

SICK

A 90-year-old Durham, North Carolina, woman was killed by at least 45 blows to her face, head, back, and chest. She suffered dozens of jagged 3-inch wounds, splintered vertebrae, shattered ribs, and torn internal organs. The alleged culprit: a 13-year-old boy who wanted to steal her car.

SICK, SICK, SICK

A 55-year-old Long Island, New York, grandmother allegedly wanted to party on New Year's Eve, but her only companion was her 5-year-old grandson. So she spent the evening dancing and feeding the tot Jell-O cubes made with vodka. Eventually, the grandson passed out and started vomiting blood. Rushed to the hospital, the lad almost died with a blood alcohol level of .252—more than twice the legal limit. Granny was arrested on charges of endangering the welfare of a minor.

BREAST-FEEDING MOM LANDS IN JAIL

A Syracuse, New York, mother called a local help line to obtain the telephone number of the nearby chapter of the La Leche League, an international organization that encourages breast-feeding—and ended up in jail. The help line transferred the call to the Syracuse Rape Crisis Center. The counselor who answered the call considered it unnatural that the woman was still breast-feeding her daughter a month short of her third birthday. So the counselor called the police, who arrested the woman on charges of incest and sexual abuse and took away her child.

The charges were soon dismissed. But the local Department of Social Services brought new charges of sex abuse and also neglect and put the daughter in foster care. Those charges were dismissed. Then the department brought still more charges. It took 350 days for the mother to be cleared and the child to be returned.

The woman is now planning to sue.

NOW SEE HERE!

A woman who sat down in the back of a Pittsburgh city bus felt like someone was staring at her. She looked around—and spotted two eyeballs lying on the seat next to her. Understandably, she became very excited and started shouting at the driver. Authorities called the county coroner, whose investigation turned up no explanation for the eyes.

THE SICKEST LOVER'S REVENGE

A 35-year-old Baltimore physician who used to work in the emergency room at Johns Hopkins Hospital was apparently furious at his ex-girlfriend—so furious that he put her name on a blood sample from an AIDS patient. You can imagine the woman's mental agony until the truth came out. The state medical board ordered the physician to perform 100 hours of community service and apologize to the woman—but is that enough?

DONALD AND DAISY DAHMER

Are your kids looking for something new to spend those allowance dollars on? Well, now they can go to their local store and read about the real-life exploits of America's most heinous killers in *Psycho Killer Comics*. The first issue chronicles the charming story of Charles Manson's bloody butchery. In one panel, a half-nude Sharon Tate begs Manson, "Please let me go. I want to live. All I want to do is have my baby."

Manson, clutching a butcher knife, replies, "Look, bitch. I have no mercy for you." Manson, of course, wasn't really at the scene of the Tate killing.

Additional issues feature such charming folks as Son of Sam killer David Berkowitz and Milwaukee cannibal Jeffrey

Dahmer. The publishers claim that the purpose of graphically telling these stories is to "promote an understanding of the tragic circumstances and events that lead to these terrible crimes."
Right.

SORE THROAT OF THE YEAR

There is dumb. There is dumber. Then there is a kind of stupidity beyond human comprehension. That rare level was reached by a Florida woman who suffers from asthma. So she kept an inhaler containing her asthma spray under her pillow—along with a loaded revolver.

You guessed it. One night she suffered an asthma attack. Half-asleep, she reached for what she thought was her inhaler, put it to her mouth, and pressed what she thought was the button to release the spray. Shortly afterward she was taken to the hospital for shooting herself in the jaw.

SICKEST SEXUAL ABUSE STORY OF THE YEAR

A 37-year-old male employee of a Tennessee nursing home was arrested for allegedly fondling an 81-year-old female patient who has a brain disease.

UNNATURAL ACTS

A 28-year-old Long Beach, California, woman was arrested after she allegedly took a 3-year-old boy from a Los Angeles day-care center, put him in a car, then set the car on fire. The boy was burned on over 60 percent of his body. The woman refused to provide any explanation for the hideous act.

MOUSE MUFFIN

At first, the woman who bit into a bran muffin purchased from a Long Island, New York, bakery thought to herself, Gee, this must have raisins in it. Then she took something hard from her mouth and discovered it was a mouse leg with some hair on it. The woman suffered vomiting, diarrhea, and high blood pressure. The Nassau County Health Department found "heavy rodent infestation" at the bakery the next day, and the woman sued for $13 million. She said, "I can't stop checking my bridgework for mouse hairs and I can't get mice out of my mind. I've baked a thousand muffins in my time, but I'll never eat another one again."

THE CASE OF THE MURDERING MAKEUP

A California computer expert was arrested on charges that he murdered his wife by poisoning her eyeliner and her coffee. According to police, the 63-year-old man extracted the poisonous mineral selenium from an AC/DC current changing device, then mixed it into his wife's Revlon eyeliner. She began to die slowly and painfully. But he allegedly grew impatient, and put a lethal dose of cyanide in her coffee.

Police closed in on the man when his ex-wife presented proof that he had tried to kill her in 1972 by lacing her coffee, tea, milk, wine, and Head & Shoulders shampoo with selenium. The ex-wife suffered skin lesions, sores, and rashes, but she agreed to drop charges when the man was referred to county mental-health services.

BASH HER, SAID THE BUS DRIVER

A 26-year-old Roanoke, Virginia, woman is still at the wheel of her school bus—despite her conviction for encouraging students on her bus to punch and kick a 17-year-old accused of having head lice. After the attack, the bus driver and her assistant bought doughnuts for the students as a reward for the violence.

SAY IT WITH FERTILIZER

A Loxahatchee, Florida, company has developed a unique new home delivery service aimed at a yet-unserved market— jilted lovers and other disgruntled people. For a fee, Poop-Poop We Do delivers a bouquet of cow manure to the object of the sender's wrath. One woman made a stink to the state health department after receiving a bouquet, but since cow manure is widely available at garden stores, the service appears headed for a "clean" bill of health.

IT WASN'T AS IF HE KILLED SOMEBODY

What he does on his own time is up to him.
—a Southern sheriff, on a deputy
charged with exposing himself to a
child while off-duty

ABUSE OF PREGNANT WOMEN
IS A NATIONAL SCANDAL

In a study reported in the *Journal of the American Medical Association*, R. Antonia Novello, Surgeon General of the United States, reports a study that revealed 37 percent of pregnant women in this country are slapped, kicked, or punched by their mates during pregnancy. Dr. Novello said the abuse strikes rich and poor women equally. And as to race? "Frequency and severity of abuse during pregnancy, as well as potential danger for homicide, were appreciably worse for white women."

MAGISTRATE HAS A WEAKNESS FOR THE SUDS

A local magistrate resigned after he admitted promising leniency to a male defendant if he could shampoo the defendant's hair. Prosecuters in the case, in which the magistrate pleaded guilty to official oppression, said the man rubbed his body against people he shampooed, giving him sexual stimulation.

WE'VE HEARD OF SHOTGUN WEDDINGS, BUT A SHOTGUN RECEPTION?

A 50-year-old Tampa, Florida, bridegroom got into a fight with his 38-year-old bride at their wedding reception. She heaved a plate of macaroni salad at him. He retaliated by pulling out a .22-caliber handgun and shooting her in the stomach.

SELF-SURGERY

A Bloomfield, New Mexico, woman whose insurance company wouldn't pay to have her silicone breast implants removed performed the surgery on herself one night after her husband and children went to bed. She took some Valium to steady her nerves, then slit herself with a razor. She managed to squeeze the silicone gel from the implants, but couldn't manage to remove the bags. The next day, a doctor removed the bags at his office.

The woman's husband said this wasn't her first attempt at self-surgery—she'd tried, unsuccessfully, to remove a wisdom tooth with a pair of pliers.

9

THE CELEBRITY
SIN-DEX

ALLEN, WOODY

The normally reclusive filmmaker and the equally publicity-shy Mia Farrow went public with a messy breakup that recorded a cataclysmic 10 on the *Scandal Annual* scandal scale. Triggering the fireworks was Allen's admitted affair with Farrow's 21-year-old adopted daughter, Soon-Yi Previn—an intimate relationship Farrow first learned about when she found nude photographs of the young woman taken in Allen's apartment. When private attempts at arriving at a custody arrangement for the couple's one biological child and two adopted children failed, both parties went public with charges and counter-charges that occupied the front pages of the New York City tabloids for weeks. Curiously, the scandal erupted just a month prior to the opening of Allen's new movie, in which he plays a college professor who has an affair with one of his young students.

BERBICK, TREVOR

The former world heavyweight boxing champion, who lost his crown when Mike Tyson knocked him out in 1986, was also sent to prison in the same year for the same charge. A jury in Miami found Berbick guilty of raping a woman who worked as a babysitter for the family.

BUSH, GEORGE

The White House budget for travel in 1992 is a modest $29,000. But the real cost, according to Congressional sources, is close to a whopping $60 million. Every time the President decides to fly to Maine for the weekend, *Air Force One* rolls up, a 747 that costs $26,000 an hour to operate. Behind the President's plane, at $9,000 an hour, is a cargo plane containing the President's bullet-proof limousine, Secret Service "war wagons," and a White House communications car. In the interest of the economy, don't you think the President could play golf in the Washington area a few weekends?

CLAPTON, ERIC

Stories about the tragic death of the singer's 4-year-old son, who fell 400 feet from the window of his mother's Manhattan apartment building, indicated that the boy was Clapton's only child. But a British inquest into the boy's death brought to light the fact that Clapton is the father of a 7-year-old girl by a married woman who lives on the Caribbean island of Montserrat. The woman and her husband raise the little blond girl.

DAHMER, JEFFREY

Of all the horrors committed by this serial killer, perhaps the most bizarre came to light this year when evidence surfaced that he attempted to turn some of his victims into zombies before he killed them. Dahmer drugged them, then performed lobotomies by drilling into their skulls and pouring various fluids inside. When his experiments failed, he strangled and dissected his victims.

DUCHESS OF YORK

Buckingham Palace stunned royalty watchers with the announcement that the former Sarah Ferguson, the Duchess of York (better known as Fergie), was separating from her husband, Prince Andrew. Then the scandal escalated dramatically when a London tabloid published graphic photographs of Fergie smooching topless with a dashing Texas millionaire—in the presence of her 2- and 4-year-old children.

Just prior to the publication of these pictures, Fergie and her husband were seen together at a number of events, leading to speculation that they were attempting to work things out. Then came the revelations that may have produced a Prince Andrew fury that matched Hurricane Andrew's fury.

GOLD, TRACEY

The actress who plays Kirk Cameron's sister on the long-running TV show "Growing Pains" checked into an eating-disorder clinic for treatment of anorexia. She had lost 32 pounds over the course of two years, and carried just 90 pounds on her 5-foot, 2-inch frame. Her father and agent, Harry Gold, told *TV Guide* that Tracey has been "struggling with anorexia for a few years."

HELMSLEY, LEONA

The Queen of Mean finally exhausted her appeals and entered the Federal Correctional System to serve her four-year sentence for tax evasion. No doubt she's learning a few housekeeping lessons she missed as head of the Helmsley hotel empire.

HITLER, ADOLF

This may come as a complete shock to you: The exalted führer of the Third Reich, leader of the noble Ayran race, evidently didn't consider taking a bath to be one of his obligations. Said former silent-screen actress Lina Basquette, commenting on Hitler's unsuccessful attempt to seduce her, "Maybe if I hadn't been so fastidious I might have changed history. But, oh, that body odor of his."

JACKSON, MICHAEL

The eccentric entertainer set U.S.–African relations back a hundred years by his behavior on a trip to the Ivory Coast. Jackson, evidently terrified by the less-than-perfect living conditions, wore a surgical mask in public and refused to shake hands or touch anyone. The impact of the visit was summed up by a commentator for an Ivory Coast newspaper, as follows:

> The American sacred beast took it upon himself to remind us we are underdeveloped, impure; our air is polluted, infested with germs. And it's not this mutant genius, this voluntary mutant, this re-created being, bleached, neither white nor black, neither man nor woman, so delicate, so frail, who will inhale it.

JAGGER, MICK

As if America's baby boomers weren't starting to feel old already, they received an additional reminder of the passage of time when the lead singer of the Rolling Stones became a grandfather.

KENNEDY, TED

Scandal Annual's favorite cover boy over the last seven years bid adieu to single life when he wed Washington lawyer Victoria Reggie. The wedding, however, was a civil ceremony: Boston's Bernard Cardinal Law issued a pronouncement banning a church wedding because Senator Kennedy is in the eyes of the church still married to his first wife, Joan. When Kennedy married, he was considered estranged from the Church and is unable to accept Holy Communion. Senator Kennedy, however, seemed to bear up under the burden of another sin quite well.

LED ZEPPELIN: FISHY SEX-PLOITS

In his book *Stairway to Heaven: Led Zeppelin Uncensored*, Richard Cole, the band's tour manager, describes some "fishy stories" that have been the subject of rumors for years. One story, which Cole calls the "Shark Episode," spawned rumors that a female fan had been tied to a bed in Seattle's Edgewater Inn and that "a shark had been used to penetrate her." According to Cole, the truth is that a 17-year-old female redhead has asked to be tied up and Cole had used a red snapper to provide stimulation. He also writes that he and another member of the group persuaded two female groupies to take a nude bath with four octopuses which, he says, "somehow instinctively knew where to place their tentacles" to send the girls into ecstasy. And you thought business trips were boring!

LUNDEN, JOAN

"I'd like to set up an audition for my wife." Phones must have been ringing off the hook at TV stations all over the country when a judge ordered "Good Morning America" anchor Joan Lunden to fork over $18,000 a month in temporary alimony to her ex-husband Michael Krause. Lunden was also ordered to pay for the mortgage, taxes, fuel, electricity, security alarms, cable television, and property insurance on the couple's Rye, New York, home, in which Krause still lives. Finally, the judge ordered Lunden to pay $25,000 to Krause's attorney and $15,000 to his accountant.

MAPLES, MARLA

The high-profile girlfriend of the higher-profile Donald made headlines again when a hidden video camera caught her publicist, 49-year-old Chuck Jones, allegedly sneaking into her apartment to steal shoes. After Maples filed a complaint, police allegedly found 40 to 50 pairs of her shoes in Jones's apartment, as well as her bras and silk panties stuffed into drawers, air vents, and closets. According to the *New York Post*, the publicist called the paper and tearfully admitted taking the shoes.

MARCOS, IMELDA

The former Philippines' first lady took some novel approaches in her campaign for the Presidency of the country. First, she tried appealing to the poor. At a Manila rally, she told several thousand impoverished followers, "I am a squatter, too. They took away all my properties. I am one of you." Then she climbed into her air-conditioned stretch limousine and returned to her $2,000 a day hotel suite.

Guess what—the approach didn't work. So Imelda's next tactic was to claim that the foundation of her husband's wealth was good luck—he stumbled upon a vast horde of gold hidden by the Japanese when they occupied the Philippines in World War II. Marcos added further that her late husband had generously sold much of the gold to help the Philippines through hard economic times in the 1960s and 1970s. The Philippine government countered by repeating evidence that Ferdinand Marcos accumulated his fortune through embezzlement and kickbacks.

Whatever the truth, the electorate evidently didn't have much sympathy for Imelda—she lost badly.

MILKEN, MICHAEL

The former king of junk bonds, now in jail for securities fraud, dropped from the ranks of billionaires after agreeing to pay a whopping $900 million fine to settle more than 200 lawsuits. But don't weep for Milken—the deal leaves him with a personal fortune of $125 million and an additional $200 to $300 million held by his wife and children. Now, don't you consider that punishment?

MONROE, MARILYN

Fascination with this actress continues three decades after her death. By the thirtieth anniversary of her demise, August 4, 1992, a total of 84 books about her had been published, with several more in the works.

These books contain increasingly spectacular charges.

The latest, a book called *Double Cross*, written by Chuck Giancana, brother of the late Chicago crime boss Sam Giancana, charges that a four-man hit team sent by the mob assassinated Monroe in hopes of exposing her romance with former Attorney General Robert Kennedy. According to Giancana, the hit team pinned the nude actress to the bed, taped her mouth, and inserted a suppository filled with Nembutal, a powerful barbiturate.

NORIEGA, MANUEL

The ex-Panamanian dictator didn't have a great year. First of all, he was sentenced to 40 years in prison after his conviction on drug-related charges. And his wife, Felicidad Noriega, was arrested at a Miami, Florida, department store on charges of grand theft for ripping buttons worth $305 off of clothes hanging on the rack. She later pled guilty to a reduced charge and made restitution.

OYL, OLIVE

The longtime (very longtime) main squeeze of Popeye the Sailor strongly asserted a woman's right to choose on the abortion issue in a comic strip penned by cartoonist Bobby London, who'd been drawing the weekday episodes since 1986. But King Features, which syndicates the comic, muffled the outspoken maiden, withdrawing the sequence and firing London. Said an angry Popeye, defending his love, "That's all I can stands, I can't stands no more."

PRINCESS ANNE

Queen Elizabeth's only daughter, whose 1989 separation from her husband, Mark Phillips, was the first in a wave of marital problems for the royal family, officially filed for divorce. The couple were married on November 14, 1973, and have two children, Peter, 14, and Zara, 10. Both Princess Anne and her husband have been romantically linked to others during their separations.

PRINCESS DIANA

The wife of the heir to the British throne spent 1992 in the eye of the biggest storm of royal gossip and scandal since King Edward VII renounced his thrown to marry American divorcée Wallace Simpson. Three best-selling books, numerous tabloid articles, and dozens of interviews with confidantes of both Princess Di and her husband, Prince Charles, provided a portrait of an extremely troubled marriage.

Sources close to the Princess described her as a woman so devastated by her husband's formality and aloofness that she developed bulimia and attempted suicide. Sources close to the Prince described him as a man driven by an immature, spoiled, temperamental wife who has no appreciation of the duties and responsibilities of a future king.

Public sentiment, as expressed in British public opinion polls, was solidly on the side of Princess Di. The aristocracy rallied around the Prince. With the two seemingly headed toward a separation, we await some incriminating pictures or other concrete evidence of infidelity in the months to come.

QUAYLE, DAN

The famous "potatoe" incident isn't the only poor spelling to haunt the Vice President. Patrons of golf legend Sam Snead's Tavern in Orlando, Florida, were reading memorabilia on the wall when they came across a note from Quayle to Snead that read: "Sam, had a great time this weekend but the the golf was lousey." So's your spelling, Danny.

REAGAN, NANCY: NANCY DEAREST

In her autobiography, *The Way I See It*, Patti Davis charged that her mother, Nancy Reagan, was a child beater who lived in a fog of tranquilizers. Davis said her mother took five or six pills daily and was prone to frequent violent rages that sometimes included physical violence. Ronald Reagan's response at the time, according to his daughter, was, "He said I was lying and he said I was crazy. I really realized I was never going to know what it would feel like to have a father."

REYNOLDS, BURT

Reynolds revealed that he had been $30 million in debt three years ago, before his new hit TV show "Evening Shade" began to air. A persistent painful infection in his jawbone led to his becoming addicted to the sleeping pill Halcion, which, he said, resulted in his inattention to his affairs and subsequently, being wiped out financially. However, Reynolds was able to negotiate a deal with CBS that gave him 50 percent ownership of "Evening Shade" along with a hefty salary. Reynolds could receive as much as $100 million when the sitcom goes into syndication.

RIVERA, GERALDO

In one of the all-time low points of television talk show history, viewers and a live audience of 250 people watched as a cosmetic surgeon removed a needleful of fat from Geraldo

Rivera's buttocks and injected it into his face to smooth out wrinkles.

RIVERS, JOAN

Rivers's syndicated talk show is taped in the same Manhattan building as is CBS's "60 Minutes." On June 16, Rivers received a letter from Susan Bieber, an assistant producer at "60 Minutes," which read, "It has been brought to my attention from a number of women at '60 Minutes' that your employees are allowing Spike [Rivers's dog] to urinate over the toilet bowls of the ninth-floor bathroom. We would appreciate it if your employees could walk your dog outside. I thank you."

Rivers sarcastically wrote back, "This is absolutely impossible, as everyone knows Spike urinates over the toilet bowls on the eighth floor." Charges were traded back and forth until "60 Minutes" producer Don Hewitt stepped in to bring peace to the bathrooms on West 57th Street.

SCHWARZENEGGER, ARNOLD

Readers of *Spy* saw all of the muscled box-office champ when the magazine published two nude pictures from the early 1970s, when Schwarzenegger was a body builder hustling for attention. The magazine's publisher said he was not originally planning on running the photographs, but was angered when the Terminator's publicist demanded that the photos not be used.

SLASH

The guitarist for the controversial rock group Guns N' Roses signed a multimillion-dollar deal to promote a brand of vodka. The brand: Black Death, a product made in Iceland which has won increasing popularity in Europe largely because of its name. Slash-Black Death sounds like a marriage made in heaven.

TRUMP, IVANA

The ex-wife of Donald Trump published her first novel, which featured the following characters:

- Katrinka Graham, a former Czechoslovakian ski champion-turned-model who moves to New York, starts running hotels, and becomes part of the social scene

- Adam Graham, her husband, a yacht-sailing tycoon whose picture appears frequently in the paper and who leaves her for another woman

- Sugar Benson, a leggy honey blonde with a Southern drawl who specializes in husband removal.

Sound familiar? They do to the Donald, who filed a lawsuit charging that Ivana's novel is a barely disguised description of their real-life marriage and breakup, and is thus a violation of their divorce agreement. Ivana counters that the book is total fiction. In this literary dispute, which will no doubt make some lawyers very rich, the court will decide.

TYSON, MIKE

Erinn Cosby, 25-year-old daughter of Bill Cosby, appeared on television's "Entertainment Tonight," "Donahue," and "Night Talk with Jane Whitney" to charge that Mike Tyson had sexually assaulted her three years before. She said the incident occurred in Tyson's New Jersey mansion. According to her, Bill Cosby angrily demanded that Tyson agree to undergo psychotherapy. However, the boxer apparently reneged on his agreement to see a shrink. And look where he ended up.